Strickland Productions presents

D0906018

CRUSHED SHELLS AND MUD

BEN MUSGRAVE

Crushed Shells and Mud was first performed at the
Southwark Playhouse, London, on 1 October 2015

CRUSHED SHELLS AND MUD

BEN MUSGRAVE

CAST
(in alphabetical order)

Vince	**Alexander Arnold**
Lydia	**Hannah Britland**
Sarah	**Laura Howard**
Derek	**Alex Lawther**
Peter	**Simon Lenagan**

Director	**Russell Bolam**
Producers	**Joe Strickland**
	Nadezhda Zhelyazkova
	Caitlin Albery Beavan
Set Designer	**Ellan Parry**
Lighting Designer	**Richard Godin**
Sound Designer	**Richard Hammarton**
Assistant Director	**Sam Greenwood**
Movement Director	**Jack Murphy**
Assistant Designer	**Ellen Richardson**
Casting Director	**Georgia Fleury Reynolds**
Stage Manager	**Arran Ainsworth**

BIOGRAPHIES

ALEXANDER ARNOLD (Vince)

Theatre includes: *Luna Gale*, *Four Minutes Twelve Seconds* (Hampstead).

Television includes: *Death in Paradise*; *Capital*; *Poldark*; *Foyle's War*; *Silk*; *What Remains*; *A Mother's Son*; *Skins*.

Film includes: *The Salvation*.

CAITLIN ALBERY BEAVAN for Moya Productions (Producer)

As Producer theatre includes: *Shivered* (Southwark Playhouse); *Third Finger, Left Hand*, *Mrs Lowry & Son*, *Boa* (Trafalgar Studios); *The Glass Supper* (Hampstead).

As Associate Producer theatre includes: *The Illusion*, *Love Girl and the Innocent* (Southwark Playhouse); *The Mentalists* (Wyndham's).

As General Manager theatre includes: *Ladybird* (The New Diorama); Interior Designers Pantomime: *Peter Pan and the Designers of the Caribbean* (Bloomsbury).

www.moyaproductions.co.uk @moyaproductions

RUSSELL BOLAM (Director)

Theatre includes: *Marriage* (Assembly); *The Titanic Orchestra* (Pleasance); *Uncle Vanya* (St James); *The Merry Wives of Windsor* (Ivan Vazov); *Three Sisters*, *The Seagull*, *Shivered* (Southwark Playhouse); *Ghost from a Perfect Place*, *In Skagway*, *The Road to Mecca* (Arcola); *The Roman Bath* (Arcola/Ivan Vazov); *Alfred* (Vineyard); *Somersaults*, *Captain Oates' Left Sock* (Finborough); *Three More Sleepless Nights*, *Fourplay* (Tristan Bates); *The Physicists* (Aphra Studio).

His comedy directing includes shows with Edinburgh Comedy Award Nominees Pappy's and The Beta Males.

Russell is a visiting director at Arts Ed, Bristol Old Vic Theatre School, Central School of Speech and Drama, East 15, Oxford School of Drama and Royal Welsh College of Music and Drama. He is also a part-time teacher at Kent University, a Globe Education Practitioner and Visiting Artist at the National Student Drama Festival.

HANNAH BRITLAND (Lydia)

Theatre includes: *Our American Cousin* (Finborough); *Hobson's Choice* (Regent's Park Open Air Theatre); *The Blue Room* (The Bridewell); *Badenheim 1939*, *Oedipus*, *On the Town*, *Richard III*, *The Country Wife*, *The Mystery Plays*, *Uncle Vanya*, *Stitching* (Guildhall School of Music and Drama).

Television includes: *Death in Paradise*; *A Gert Lush Christmas*; *Scrotal Recall*; *Fresh Meat*; *Our World War*; *Home and Away*; *Skins: Rise*; *Big Bad World*; *Uncle*; *Vera*; *Misfits*.

Film includes: *The Hard Way* (short); *Between Two Worlds*; *Still Romance*; *Ivory Stage*; *The Best Offer*; *Rush*.

RICHARD GODIN (Lighting Designer)

Theatre includes: *JOHN* (Lyttelton, National Theatre/international tour); Michael Clark's *The Barrowlands Project* (Closing of the Cultural Olympiad, Glasgow); *No Sweat* (Cirque en Chantier, Paris/The Curve, Den Hagg/tour); Tim Key (Duchess/Soho/tour); *Money the Gameshow* (Bush/tour); *Three Little Pigs* (Salisbury/tour); *A Midsummer Night's Dream*, *Diary of a Nobody*, *Travels With my Aunt* (Royal & Derngate); *Top Girls*, *A Slight Ache*, *The Lover*, *Under Milk Wood* (Mercury, Colchester); *Twelfth Night*, *From a Jack to a King*, *Dick Barton* (Queen's, Hornchurch); *Speakout* (English Touring Opera); *Henry V* (Chichester Festival Theatre); *The Diva in Me* (Brighton Pavilion/Greenwich); *Frankenstein* (UK tour); *OneFourSeven* (Birmingham Rep/Bristol Old Vic); *On the Air* (Circus Space).

Other credits include: Goldie & The Heritage Orchestra – *Timeless* (Festival Hall, Bristol Harbourside); Michael Clark (Glastonbury Pyramid Stage); Once Upon a Castle – Castle Site Specific (Gassbeek, Belgium); Stella McCartney & Erdem Green Carpet Challenge (Wallace Collection & The Royal Institute, London); Live Transmission – Joy Division Re Worked by The Heritage Orchestra (Royal Festival Hall/Bremen/tour).

SAM GREENWOOD (Assistant Director)

Theatre includes: *Streets* (Venue 34); *Foxfinder*, *The Infant* (Nottingham New Theatre); *Homemade Fusion* (The Den).

RICHARD HAMMARTON (Sound Designer)

Theatre includes: *The Crucible* (Royal Exchange Theatre); *Sunspots*, *Deposit* (Hampstead); *Comrade Fiasco* (Gate); *Grimm Tales 2* (Bargehouse, Oxo Tower Wharf); *Beached* (Marlowe/Soho); *Ghost from a Perfect Place* (Arcola); *The Crucible* (Old Vic); *Dealer's Choice* (Royal & Derngate); *Kingston 14* (Theatre Royal Stratford East); *A Number* (Nuffield/Young Vic); *Fault Lines, I Know How I Feel About Eve* (Hampstead Downstairs); *Early Days (of a Better Nation)* (Battersea Arts Centre); *Sizwe Bansi is Dead* (Young Vic/UK tour); *Cheese* (Fanshen); *An Inspector Calls* (Theatre by the Lake); *Brilliant Adventures* (Royal Exchange Theatre); *What Happens in the Winter* (Upswing); *Bandages* (TEG Productions); *The Last Summer* (Gate, Dublin); *Mudlarks* (Hightide Festival/Theatre503/Bush); *The Taming of the Shrew* (Shakespeare's Globe); *The Pitchfork Disney* (Arcola); *Judgement Day* (The Print Room); *Same Same, Little Baby Jesus, Fixer* (Ovalhouse); *Edward II, Dr Faustus* (Royal Exchange Theatre); *Persuasion, The Constant Wife, Les Liaisons Dangereuses, Arsenic and Old Lace, The Real Thing, People at Sea* (Salisbury Playhouse); *Platform* (Old Vic Tunnels); *Ghosts* (Duchess); *Pride and Prejudice* (Bath Theatre Royal/national tour); *Speaking in Tongues* (Duke of York's); *The Mountaintop* (Theatre503/Trafalgar 1); *The Rise and Fall of Little Voice* (Harrogate); *A Raisin in the Sun* (Lyric Hammersmith/tour); *The Shooky, Dealer's Choice* (Birmingham Rep); *Hello and Goodbye, Some Kind of Bliss* (Trafalgar 2); *Six Characters Looking For an Author* (Young Vic); *Breakfast with Mugabe* (Ustinov, Bath Theatre Royal); *Someone Who'll Watch Over Me*

(Royal & Derngate); *Inches Apart, Natural Selection, Salt Meets Wound, Ship of Fools* (Theatre503); Steve Nallon's *Christmas Carol* (The Door, Birmingham Rep); *Blowing* (national tour/Fanshen).

Television includes: *Ripper Street*; Agatha Christie's *Marple: The Secret of Chimneys*; Agatha Christie's *Marple; No Win No Fee; Sex 'N' Death; Wipeout; The Ship; Primeval; Dracula; Jericho; If I Had You; A History of Britain; Silent Witness; Daiziel and Pascoe; Alice Through the Looking Glass*.

Film includes: *The Pier* (short); *First the Worst* (short); *Raptured; A Neutral Corner; Konigsspitz* (short); *K2* (short); *The Fisherman's Wife* (short); *Snow the Button* (short); *The Nine Lives of Thomas Katz; Scenes of a Sexual Nature*.

Other credits include: Foundling Museum (The Foundling Museum); Moore Outside (Tate Britain); *You Shall Go to the Ball* (Royal Opera House); *Light* (BAC).

LAURA HOWARD (Sarah)

Theatre includes: *Invincible* (Orange Tree/St James); *Lost in Yonkers* (Watford Palace Theatre); *The Norman Conquests* (Liverpool Playhouse); *Life of Riley* (Stephen Joseph Theatre/UK tour); *Communicating Doors* (Stephen Joseph Theatre); *Two Women* (Theatre Royal Stratford East); *Look Back in Anger* (Northern Stage); *The Blue Room* (Anvil Arts); *Switzerland* (HighTide); *Dracula* (Centerline/English Touring Consortium); *The Hotel in Amsterdam* (Donmar Warehouse); *Emma* (Good Company); *Arcadia* (Chichester Festival Theatre); *The Master Builder, The Taming of the Shrew* (English Touring Theatre).

Television includes: *Cuffs; The Delivery Man; Doctors; Casualty; Young Dracula; EastEnders; Doctors; Midsomer Murders; Cold Enough for Snow; Soldier Soldier; Eskimo Day; Covington Cross*.

Film includes: *Get Well Soon* (short); *The Responsibility Virgin* (short); *Queen's Park Story* (short).

ALEX LAWTHER (Derek)

Theatre includes: *The Glass Supper, Fault Lines* (Hampstead); *South Downs* (Harold Pinter/Chichester); *Casting* (Young Vic; workshop); *Oppenheimer* (RSC; workshop).

Television includes: *Virtuoso*.

Film includes: *Departure; Narrated By* (short); *The Imitation Game; X+Y; Benjamin Britten: Peace & Conflict*.

Radio includes: *How to Say Goodbye Properly* by EV Crowe; *Rock me Amadeus; The Cazalets*.

SIMON LENAGAN (Peter)

Theatre includes: *Shivered* (Southwark Playhouse); *Normal* (Union); *Penetrator* (Old Red Lion); *Macbeth* (Westcliff); *The Way of the World* (Royal Exchange Theatre); *Stand-Up* (Old Red Lion/Edinburgh); *Room at the Top* (King's Head); *The Greenhouse Effect* (Riverside Studios); *The Long and the Short and the Tall* (Noël Coward); *Punch Junkies* (Shaw).

Television includes: *Partners in Crime; Londongrad; Outnumbered; Survivors; The Palace; Holby Blue; The Time of Your Life; Spooks; Heartbeat; Holby City; May 33rd; Coronation Street; Messiah II; Outside the Rules; Monarch of the Glen; Other People's Children; This is Personal: The Hunt for the Yorkshire Ripper; Pure Wickedness; The Grand.*

Film includes: *Spectre; Born of War; WMD; Run Fatboy Run; Basic Instinct 2; Passer By; Bring Me Your Love.*

BEN MUSGRAVE (Playwright)

Theatre includes: *Across the Dark Water* (The Point, Eastleigh, UK tour); *Politrix* (Hackney Showrooms); *Stunted Trees and Broken Bridges, Breathing Country* (nominated for Brian Way Award; Y Touring Theatre, UK tour); *His Teeth, Pancras Boys Club* (Only Connect); *Boars and Dragonflies* (Miniaturists/Arcola); *Exams are Getting Easier* (Birmingham Repertory Theatre); *Pretend You Have Big Buildings* (Royal Exchange Theatre; winner, Bruntwood Prize).

Television includes: *Beginner's Call; The Local Man* (under option, Lime Pictures).

Radio includes: *The British Club.*

ELLAN PARRY (Set Designer)

Theatre includes: *Lesere* (Jermyn Street); *Snow White* (London Children's Ballet); *Posh* (Nottingham Playhouse/Salisbury Playhouse); *Milked, Each Slow Dusk* (Pentabus); *The Nightmares of Carlos Fuentes* (Arcola); *Someone Who'll Watch Over Me* (The Theatre, Chipping Norton); *A Midsummer Night's Dream* (Tooting Arts Club); *The Miser* (Watermill); *The Wind in the Willows* (Taunton Brewhouse); *Other Hands* (Riverside Studios/UK tour); *Without You, Pippin* (Mernier Chocolate Factory); *Sense and Sensibility* (UK tour); *Don Juan Comes Home From the War* (Finborough); *Electric Hotel* (Sadler's Wells); *Gutted* (Assembly Productions); *Plucker* (Southwark Playhouse); *Katy Brand's Big Ass Live Show* (Leicester Square Theatre/UK tour).

Opera includes: *El Nino* (Spoleto Opera Festival); *Neige* (Les Theatres de la Ville de Luxembourg); *Iernin* (Surrey Opera); *Noye's Fludd* (Southbank Centre); *The Secret Marriage* (British Youth Opera); *I Lombardi* (University College Opera); *Autumn Opera Scenes* (Guildhall School of Music and Drama); *Great Expectations* (Royal College of Music); *The Fairy Queen* (Brighton Theatre Royal/Brighton Early Music Festival); *Carmen* (Sadler's Wells); *The Magic Flute* (City Music Services, Glyndebourne); *Albert Herring, Giustino, Les Dialogues de Carmelites* (Trinity-Laban); *Carmen* (Blackheath Opera).

NADEZHDA ZHELYAZKOVA (Producer)

Theatre includes: *Sinfonia Erasmus* (FITEI, Portugal); *Las Maravillas: the Lost Souls of Mictlan* (London Horror Festival); *Crave* (Zlomvaz Festival, Prague Quadrennial 2015); *Dickens Abridged* (Edinburgh Fringe/UK tour); *The Tobolowsky Files* (Edinburgh Fringe).

Nadezhda has worked for the Asia Triennial Manchester 2011, Create Salford 2013, and was a Production Placement at the London International Festival of Theatre for LIFT 2014.

'Southwark Playhouse churn out arresting productions at a rate of knots' *Time Out*

Southwark Playhouse is all about telling stories and inspiring the next generation of storytellers and theatre-makers. It aims to facilitate the work of new and emerging theatre practitioners from early in their creative lives to the start of their professional careers.

Through our schools work we aim to introduce local people at a young age to the possibilities of great drama and the benefits of using theatre skills to facilitate learning. Each year we engage with over 5,000 school pupils through free schools performances and long-term in school curriculum support.

Through our Young Company (YoCo), a youth-led theatre company for local people between the ages of 14–25, we aim to introduce young people to the many and varied disciplines of running a semi-professional theatre company. YoCo provides a training ground to build confidence and inspire young people towards a career in the arts.

Our theatre programme aims to facilitate and showcase the work of some of the UK's best up-and-coming talent with a focus on reinterpreting classic plays and contemporary plays of note. Our two atmospheric theatre spaces enable us to offer theatre artists and companies the opportunity to present their first fully realised productions. Over the past 22 years we have produced and presented early productions by many aspiring theatre practitioners many of whom are now enjoying flourishing careers.

What People Say...

'High-achieving, life-giving spirit' Fiona Mountford, *Evening Standard*

'The revitalised Southwark Playhouse' Lyn Gardner, *Guardian*

'I love that venue so much. It is, without doubt, one of the most exciting theatre venues in London.' Philip Ridley, Playwright

For more information about our forthcoming season and to book tickets visit **www.southwarkplayhouse.co.uk.** You can also support us online by joining our Facebook and Twitter pages.

STAFF LIST

CRUSHED SHELLS AND MUD

Ben Musgrave

Acknowledgements

The idea for this play began on a trip to Uganda to talk to people whose lives had been transformed by antiretroviral drugs. Many thanks to Annie Katuregye and all who took the time to tell me about their experiences. Thanks also to Theatrescience, Rebecca Gould, and Caroline Grundy for developing the idea and for getting me out there in the first place.

I wrote the first draft of the play on attachment at the National Theatre Studio and I am enormously grateful to all at the Studio who enabled this – in particular Brian Walters, Matthew Poxon, and Rebecca Frecknall (who directed two excellent workshop readings of the play, the first featuring Nick Blakeley, Robin Pearce and Jess Murphy, the second Siân Thomas, Ted Reilly, Tom Hughes and Lou Broadbent).

I am always indebted to the Dog House Group – Matt Morrison, Robin Booth, Samantha Ellis, and Nick Harrop. And also to Rachel Taylor, Robert Holman, and Lucy Morrison for useful thoughts. Thank you to Kirsten Forster. Thank you also to all at Nick Hern Books and the Southwark Playhouse.

Huge thank you to Joe Strickland, Simon Lenegan, and especially to Russell Bolam who believed in the play and had the cheek and sheer bloody-mindedness to get it on.

To my parents for supporting this play and my strange career, and of course to Selene Burn, for everything.

B.M.

Characters

DEREK, *seventeen*
LYDIA, *seventeen*
VINCENT, *seventeen*
SARAH, *forty-eight*
PETER, *forty*
OLD LADY, *seventy-five*

Notes

The play can be performed with a cast of five actors, doubling Sarah and the Old Lady.

A forward slash (/) marks an interruption by the next speaker.

The absence of a full stop at the end of a line marks a trailing off or an interruption of thought.

This text went to press before the end of rehearsals and so may differ slightly from the play as performed.

ACT ONE

Scene One

She Crawled Out of the Sea

The east coast of England.

A field. High brambles, nettles, tall grasses obscure a view of the sea. The memory of a path down.

In the other direction, a track leading to the village.

Within the field a holiday caravan, weathered, battered, seagull-spattered.

A changeable day in summer. At this moment it is grey.

DEREK *emerges from the caravan, carrying a plain brown notebook. He goes to the side of the caravan, and climbs up the side-ladder.*

From the top, he looks at the sea for a moment, then sits down, dangling his legs from the roof.

He takes the notebook, and makes a slight adjustment to what is written within.

He starts to read what he has out loud.

DEREK   One day she came out of the sea.
                She crawled out of the mud, quietly.
                Shy and beautiful
                Brushing off sand and shells.

                And over marsh and pool she looked straight into his eyes.
                And even from that distance
                He knew she understood him.
                And knew she had the answers
                To all the things that hurt or didn't make sense.

                He looks up as the sun comes out and warms his face.

Scene Two

Lydia

By the caravan.

A brighter day.

DEREK *is showing* LYDIA *around.*

He is not in her league.

DEREK   (*Of the path to the sea.*) Now, normally you can get to the sea this way, there's a path that winds down, but there haven't been the walkers really, in recent years.
So it's quite grown over.

I'll see if I can beat it back at the weekend.

LYDIA   (*Smiling.*) Don't worry.

DEREK   Oh I don't mind!

LYDIA   It was just a whim.

DEREK   We need to keep it open.
It's a right of way.
You can't just let it go.

(*Of the caravan.*) This is just...

Someone just dumped this here.
We use it sometimes – the farmer doesn't mind.

You're most welcome at any time.

LYDIA   Thanks.

DEREK *tries to point out the view.*

DEREK   Well, that's the sea.
(*Looking down into the vegetation.*) It's not a great beach, if I'm honest.
Quite muddy.
There's a better one further down the coast.
Rockpools, a bit of sand.
I could show you?

LYDIA   (*Smiling.*) Okay.

DEREK	I'm not much of a swimmer. Well, I can thrash about...
	(*Of her name*.) It was 'Lydia' wasn't it?
LYDIA	Yes.
DEREK	(*Embarrassed*.) I always forget in the flurry of it. And then it's embarrassing to ask again.
	Pause.
	(*Of his name*.) Derek.
LYDIA	Yes.
	LYDIA *smiles. They look into the brambles.*
DEREK	Did you swim where you were before?
LYDIA	A little bit.
DEREK	Where was it?
	Beat.
LYDIA	Sussex.
DEREK	So this must be a bit of a change!
LYDIA	Yes!
DEREK	Everything okay there?
LYDIA	Yes, we were fine.
	Pause.
DEREK	Your parents move out here?
LYDIA	No... They're in... Germany.
	Business...
	I'm staying with my aunt for the holidays.
	LYDIA *stares out.*
DEREK	(*Of the whole area*.) There's not much here.
	It's not Well it's not too wonderful.

If you're after clubs and things there's one in
Stonesea. We had a disco at the village hall last
year but it wasn't up to much.

There's a shop or two and a pub.

I think it would be hard in a new place.

LYDIA *looks down. She suddenly appears upset.*

I don't know I'd have the bravery to be honest.

He tries, inexpertly, to comfort her.

Don't worry, you'll be alright. You'll be as right
as rain!

Pause. He can think of only one solution.

I can do you a cup of tea?

Pause.

(*Of the caravan.*) I've got a thing rigged up in
here.

LYDIA   Okay, thanks.

DEREK   Maybe you have to go?

LYDIA   No, I'm okay for a bit.

DEREK   Right!
             I'll go and get it on.
             (*Of the tea.*) It might have to be black I'm afraid.

             DEREK *opens the caravan door and goes in.*

             LYDIA *takes a cigarette from a soft anonymous
             packet and lights it.*

             She looks around as she smokes.

             (*From inside.*) There we go!

             DEREK *comes out. He sees her smoking. A
             moment of alarm.*

LYDIA   Sorry

DEREK   No, don't worry!

LYDIA   Am I not allowed?

DEREK   Course, I just didn't know you / did

LYDIA   (*Offering him one.*) Would you like / one?

DEREK   (*Smiling.*) No, thank you!

             Beat.

             I've never taken to it.

             Pause.

             (*Going back into the caravan for the tea.*) I'll just get the

             (*From inside.*) Do you want sugar?

LYDIA   No.

             Pause. DEREK *comes out.*

DEREK   Will you promise me something, Lydia?

             Will you give up by the time you're twenty-five?

LYDIA   If I last till twenty-five.

             Beat.

DEREK   Why do you say that?

             Beat. LYDIA *realises she has said something odd.*

LYDIA   Sorry, I was being dramatic.

DEREK   Are you often dramatic?

LYDIA   No, not really.

             Beat. She extinguishes her cigarette. DEREK *goes into the caravan to get the tea.*

             She checks her phone.

DEREK   Reception comes and goes I'm afraid...

             She puts her phone away.

It's got markedly worse, actually, the mast is often broken, and they take weeks to repair it.

Beat.

Sorry, I know I go on a bit.

LYDIA   No, you're alright.

VINCENT*, enters, unseen. He is smart in a way* DEREK *is not.*

VINCENT   Can I smell tobacco in the air?

DEREK *freezes.*

DEREK   No.

VINCENT   It wasn't you, was it, Derek?

DEREK   No, mate.

VINCENT   You weren't smoking were you?

DEREK   No!

DEREK *shrinks back.*

LYDIA   It was me.

VINCENT   Hello.

LYDIA   Hello.

VINCENT   Have you got a spare one?

LYDIA   Sure.

She goes to her bag, and searches for her cigarettes. DEREK *disapproves of* VINCENT.

VINCENT   (*To* DEREK.) What's the problem, chicken, it's only a cigarette?

DEREK   She doesn't have to.

LYDIA   I don't mind.

VINCENT   (*To* LYDIA.) You're here on your holidays?

LYDIA   Yeah.

VINCENT   I saw you in the village.

           LYDIA *hands him a cigarette.*

           Thanks.

           Derek's been showing you round?

LYDIA   Yeah.

VINCENT   He's made you a brew?
           Isn't he fantastic!

DEREK   No!

VINCENT   You could polish him up and put him on a ring!

           LYDIA *smiles.*

           He knows all the places!
           We all *love* Derek, don't we?

           DEREK *looks away.*

           What's your name?

LYDIA   (*Smiling.*) Lydia.

VINCENT   (*Holding out his hand to shake hers.*) Pleased to
           meet you, Lydia.

           She shakes his hand.

DEREK   This is Vince.

VINCENT   Vincent.

           LYDIA *doesn't flinch from his gaze.*

           There's a pub in the village, Lydia.

LYDIA   Yeah?

VINCENT   There are lock-ins, parties. People come from
           miles around.

           Beat.

           There's one tonight.

LYDIA   Not tonight.

VINCENT   Why not?

LYDIA   I can't, tonight.

VINCENT   Can I try and persuade you?

DEREK   She doesn't want to go with you, Vince!

VINCENT   She didn't say that.

LYDIA   No, I didn't say that.

Beat.

(*To* DEREK.) Are you going?

DEREK   No.

VINCENT   He's most welcome.

DEREK   I'm alright.

Beat.

VINCENT   Can I have a cup of tea, Derek?

Pause. DEREK *seems anxious about leaving* VINCENT *and* LYDIA *together.*

No, I'll go, don't worry.

DEREK   You can have mine.

VINCENT   You sure?

DEREK   Yeah.

VINCENT   Thanks!

(*To* LYDIA.) He doesn't like people in his caravan.

DEREK   I don't mind!

VINCENT   (*About going to the pub.*) Do you like dancing, Lydia?

LYDIA   Yes.

VINCENT   I can tell.

LYDIA   How?

VINCENT   How about we go to the pub?

LYDIA	I need to get home.
VINCENT	Where do you live? I'll walk you.
LYDIA	No, I'm fine.
VINCENT	Where are you, though?

She gestures imprecisely.

LYDIA	Over that way.
VINCENT	You want to be careful on the paths at night.
LYDIA	Why?
VINCENT	There could be shrinkies out.

Beat. LYDIA *is alarmed.*

DEREK	What? There aren't, Lydia!
VINCENT	There are!
DEREK	Not round here.
VINCENT	It's coming our way, they say! Woman died last week in Leigh – a cockle-picker. They say it was that.
DEREK	(*Uncertain.*) Don't be stupid!
VINCENT	They say it's coming.
DEREK	It won't get here.
VINCENT	Did it get to where you were, Lydia?
LYDIA	No.
VINCENT	They say there's more of them about than we would think.

Pause.

Well, you be careful.

LYDIA	I will.
VINCENT	Are you after anything else, Lydia? Medicinals?

Beat. LYDIA *is alarmed.*

Something to make you feel good?

Then she understands what he means.

LYDIA   What can you get here?

VINCENT   (*Ushering her away.*) Not in front of Derek.

DEREK   It's alright!

VINCENT   Derek doesn't approve of drugs.

DEREK   It's not that!

VINCENT   He doesn't approve of my lifestyle.

DEREK   (*Trying to save face.*) It's not that.

LYDIA   I don't think he liked me smoking.

DEREK   No, / I didn't mean

VINCENT   (*To* DEREK.) Cheeky bleeder!

           VINCENT *'lightheartedly' smears his hand up
           against* DEREK*'s nose.*

DEREK   Getoff!

VINCENT   You leave the lady alone.

DEREK   I didn't do anything!

VINCENT   (*To* LYDIA, *of* DEREK.) He gives you any jip,
           you box him round the ears, that's what I do.

           VINCENT *shadow-boxes with* DEREK. DEREK
           tries to shadow-box back but it's hopeless.
           DEREK *grins and breaks it off.*

           VINCENT *grins at* LYDIA.

           Isn't he a little diamond?

           Beat.

           Come out tonight, Lydia!

LYDIA   Another time.

VINCENT   When would suit?

LYDIA   I'll let you know.

VINCENT   I'll ask you again.

LYDIA   (*Smiling.*) You do that.

               Beat. VINCENT *looks at his phone.*

VINCENT   (*Making to hug her.*) Now, I've got business to
               attend to, so it's nice to meet you.

LYDIA   (*Accepting the hug.*) Yeah, nice to meet you.

VINCENT   Thanks for the smoke.

               LYDIA *smiles.*

               VINCENT *turns and exits.*

               She watches after him.

LYDIA   He's cheeky, isn't he?

DEREK   Yeah.

               I'll have to have words with him, about that.
               With you just got here.

LYDIA   Don't worry about me.

DEREK   He thinks he can say whatever he wants!
               You don't have to accept it.
               You don't have to have anything to do with him,
               if you don't want to.

LYDIA   It's okay.

               Pause.

DEREK   He can be a bully, sometimes.
               His dad

               His dad hasn't been very good.

               Pause.

LYDIA   I should be getting back.

DEREK   Would you like a view of the sea before you go?

               (*Of the caravan.*) You can see from the top of this.

DEREK scrambles round the side of the caravan, then climbs up the side-ladder to demonstrate.

LYDIA   It's rusty.

DEREK   Oh, it's quite safe.

LYDIA climbs up. She sees the sea. She smiles.

It's nice when the sun's on it, isn't it?

The sunsets are often

She seems to be going within herself.

You've got to get home.

Sensitively, he gets down the ladder. She finishes looking at the sea, then begins to climb down.

On her descent, she cuts her finger on a jag on one of the ladder rungs.

LYDIA   Ow.

DEREK   Are you alright?

LYDIA   Yes, fine, I just

She licks her finger.

DEREK   Oh god / I'm

LYDIA   It's alright.

Beat.

DEREK   I'm sorry about that.

LYDIA   It's fine.

DEREK   Would you like a plaster?

LYDIA   No, really

Beat. Pause.

DEREK   I'll try to beat the path through tomorrow.

LYDIA   Please don't go to any effort.

DEREK   No, I will.

LYDIA   It was just something to say…
           About wanting to see the sea.
           It's not important.

           Pause.

DEREK   Lydia

           DEREK *notices that* LYDIA*'s hand is bleeding.*

           (*Reaching out to take her hand.*) Lydia, your /
           hand

LYDIA   (*Looking down in fright.*) Oh

DEREK   It's bleeding quite a bit.

           *Quite instantly, he takes out a clean white
           handkerchief, and wipes the blood off. She
           instantly pulls away.*

LYDIA   No!

DEREK   Sorry / I just

LYDIA   (*Panicking.*) Don't touch it!

           DEREK *in the headlights.*

           (*Of the handkerchief.*) Don't touch it! Get rid of it!

           He throws it on the floor confused.

           Pause. She calms.

           (*Calming down.*) Sorry

DEREK   (*Gently.*) It's okay.

LYDIA   (*Back to normal.*)
           Sorry, I was

           I have a phobia about it. Blood.

DEREK   Okay.

LYDIA   It's nothing really. It passes.

DEREK   I understand.

LYDIA   I really must go.

DEREK	(*Of the rusty ladder*.) I'm sorry about the
LYDIA	No, it was my fault.
DEREK	I'll have to see to that.
LYDIA	Do people come here, much, Derek?
DEREK	No, not very much.

Pause. She makes to go off, then turns.

LYDIA   Derek

Derek, thank you, for being kind.

Pause. She exits down the track.

DEREK *watches her go, and then looks at the ladder for the offending jag. He flakes it off.*

He picks up the blooded handkerchief, and puts it in his notebook, like he's pressing a flower.

It is getting dark.

The sound of the sea.

Scene Three

Peter

By the caravan. A hot day.

The path down to the sea has noticeably widened.

PETER *enters, carrying a briefcase.*

PETER   Hello?

Hello?

Anyone about?

PETER *puts down his briefcase, then flings open the door of the caravan, but there's no one in there.*

PETER *goes into the caravan.*

> DEREK *emerges up the sea path, sweating. His shirt is unbuttoned, and he carries a machete.*

DEREK   Who's there?

Is there someone

> PETER *stumbles out of the caravan.* DEREK *and* PETER *freeze,* DEREK *with his machete raised.*

PETER   Christ.

DEREK   Sorry.

PETER   You gave me a shock.

DEREK   (*Keeping the machete raised.*) I'm sorry, sir.

PETER   (*Of the machete.*) Put it down, then.

> DEREK *puts the machete down.*

You shouldn't spring on a man with a weapon, you don't know what he could do.

Pause.

I must have come the wrong way, I was looking for the pub.

DEREK   It's back up the track.

PETER   (*Of the machete.*) What you doing with that?

DEREK   The path.
Down to the beach.

PETER   What about it?

DEREK   I was beating it back.

PETER   Why?

DEREK   It was all grown over.

PETER   You're keeping it open?

DEREK   Yes.

PETER   The walkers don't come no more?

DEREK   I'm afraid not.

Pause. PETER *takes the machete and examines it.*

PETER   (*Of the machete.*) This is blunt.

DEREK   I know.

PETER   The blade is blunt.

DEREK   I'm sorry.

PETER   We'll get it sharp for you.

Beat.

(*Looking down the path.*). You've done all that with a blade like this?

DEREK   It's been a bit of a job.

PETER   Fuckin hell.

DEREK   Yeah!

PETER   It's a good deed.

PETER *tosses the machete onto the grass.*

What's your name?

DEREK   Derek.

PETER   When the time comes, Derek, we're going to need boys like you.

DEREK   What time?

PETER   You'll know.

DEREK   I don't.

PETER   You will.

Pause.

This your den?

DEREK   Not really.

PETER   Your little place?

DEREK   I suppose so.

PETER   Your parents know you hide here?

Beat.

DEREK   They don't care.

PETER   (*Of the place*.) You love it?

DEREK   Yes.

PETER   Yeah, I can see that.

Pause.

It's a beautiful part of the country.

If only you knew how far we're still to fall.

There've been cases now twenty miles from here.
It's getting closer.
It's gonna be like London was.

And nobody does anything about it.

Am I boring you?

DEREK   No.

PETER   This is real, do you understand?

Pause.

You got a good nose on you?

DEREK   I think so.

PETER   Good eyes?

DEREK   Twenty twenty.

PETER   Will you do us a favour, Derek?

Keep your eyes open?
Anything unusual?
People acting strangely?

Will you do that for me, Derek?

DEREK   Yes, sir.

PETER   This is for the country. This is for good decent people.

Pause. PETER *offers* DEREK *a fiver.*

Look, there's a fiver.
Buy yourself some chips.

Go on... no strings attached.

DEREK   No, I'm alright.

PETER   Just go on.

Beat. DEREK *takes the money.*

You'll find me in the village.
I'm speaking tonight. At the pub.

You see anything, you let me know.

DEREK   Okay.

VINCENT enters.

VINCENT   Who's this?

PETER   I'm from the League.
(*To* VINCENT.) I was just telling your friend
about my talk.

VINCENT   I heard about it.

PETER   Maybe I'll see you there.

VINCENT   Maybe.

Pause. PETER *exits.*

If I want to die of boredom.

VINCENT sees the machete.

You've been beating back the path?

DEREK   Yeah.

*VINCENT picks up the machete. Pause. He looks
at DEREK.*

VINCENT   Come here.

Come here.

DEREK   What are you gonna do?

VINCENT   No, I'm not going to do anything!

DEREK   You sure?

VINCENT   I promise.

DEREK   That's what you always say.

VINCENT   I promise you.

DEREK goes over to VINCENT.

Kneel.

DEREK   No.

VINCENT   Go on, kneel.

Pause. DEREK kneels down. VINCENT
'knights' him with the machete, the blade
touching the skin. DEREK is scared.

Arise, Sir Derek.

Pause. DEREK doesn't arise.

Why don't you get up?

Pause.

DEREK   I'm frightened.

VINCENT   Why are you frightened?

(*Angering.*) Why are you frightened?

He gets the machete against DEREK's neck.

Don't say things like that, Derek, it'll make
things worse.

Don't be frightened of me – do you know how
shit that makes me feel?

Pause.

Is she here?

DEREK   Who?

Pause.

VINCENT   You know who.

DEREK   Lydia?

VINCENT   Yes, Lydia.

DEREK   No.

VINCENT   Are you in love with her?

DEREK   No!

VINCENT   Would you like to hold her hand?

DEREK   Vince!

VINCENT   Give her little feather-kisses.

DEREK   Shut up!

VINCENT   And read her poetry?

DEREK   No!

VINCENT   Read her poetry and then take her into that caravan, and try to

             VINCENT *pushes* DEREK *hard, against the side of the caravan, then pins him there.*

             Find a way in.

             VINCENT *pushes his hand up* DEREK*'s face, smearing his nose.*

DEREK   Get off!

VINCENT   (*Forcing against* DEREK.) Try and pop / your

DEREK   Getoff / Vince!

VINCENT   Try and pop your little chap in!

             Beat. VINCENT *lets* DEREK *go.*

             I'm really sorry, Derek, that was inappropriate.

             Pause.

             I'm sorry, I really am.

DEREK   Are you alright, mate?

VINCENT   Yeah.

DEREK   Is it your dad?

             How are you feeling?

VINCENT   Oh fuck off, Derek.

             Just fuck off.

             LYDIA *enters*.

LYDIA   Hi.

DEREK   Hi.

VINCENT   Your man's been beating back the path.

DEREK   Should be able to get down, now.

             LYDIA *goes over to the path and looks down to
             the sea*.

LYDIA   It must have been a lot of work!

DEREK   It needed doing.

             Beat.

             I was thinking of having a swim.

LYDIA   I don't have my kit.

DEREK   Another time, perhaps?

VINCENT   (*To* LYDIA.) I've got something for you, as it
             happens.

             *Pause. He gets out a brown paper bag containing
             some weed*.

             It's sweet.

LYDIA   Yeah?

VINCENT   Like you.

             LYDIA *smiles, shaking her head – 'that old one'*.

             (*To* DEREK.) Can we go inside the caravan?

             Do you mind, Derek?

DEREK   Not at all.

VINCENT   Are you sure?

DEREK   Let me just clear some things.

VINCENT   Don't trouble yourself, mate.

            DEREK *goes in*. VINCENT *turns to* LYDIA.

VINCENT   He's tidying away his writing.

LYDIA   I'm sorry?

VINCENT   He does his writing in there.

LYDIA   Oh!

DEREK   (*Popping his head round the door*.) What?

VINCENT   I was saying you do your writing in there.

DEREK   (*Embarrassed*.) Not really.

VINCENT   Nothing to be embarrassed about!

LYDIA   What writing do you do, Derek?

DEREK   (*Embarrassed*.) Do you want the light on?

LYDIA   No / it's fine.

DEREK   I'll put it on.

            DEREK *goes back in, and turns the light on*.

            Pause. He comes out.

            It's ready.

            VINCENT *goes inside*. LYDIA *goes to the door*.

LYDIA   (*Of the weed*.) Come and join us, Derek?

            Pause. DEREK *outside*.

DEREK   No I'm okay.

VINCENT   (*From inside*.) Derek, we might be some time!

            DEREK *and* LYDIA.

DEREK   I need to get back, anyway.
          Do the tea.

          Maybe I'll see you soon?

          Pause.

LYDIA   Yeah, we should...

DEREK   I could show you the pools.

LYDIA   (*Heartbreakingly non-committal.*) Sure.

DEREK   I can do most times.

LYDIA   Okay.

          Pause. DEREK *has prewritten his number on a
          piece of paper. He gives it to her.*

DEREK   This is my number, if you need anything.

          She takes it. Smiles.

          I'll see you around, anyway.

LYDIA   Yeah.

          Pause.

DEREK   Have a good night.

          Pause.

LYDIA   Have a good night, Derek.

          *She goes into the caravan. Pause. The sun.
          The sea. The sound of it.* DEREK *exits.*

Scene Four

A Meditation

In the darkness, a recording: the voice of the OLD LADY.
A meditation.

OLD LADY   I've got my heart.
I've got my heart.
I've got my blood.
I've got my blood.
I've got my wings.
I've seen the way.

I'm going to be born.
I'm going to be born any day.

Any day this search will be over.
Any day I'll find you.
And take you home.

Scene Five

Seeing

A few days later.

By the caravan. Dusk.

LYDIA *enters, from the path, anxious that she's been followed.*
She looks around. She knocks on the door of the caravan.
Nobody answers. So she goes in. She turns the light on. Now
she can be seen through one of the windows.

DEREK *enters from the track.*

LYDIA *unbuttons her blouse.*
There is a dark mark on her belly.
She examines it. She feels the burden of something. She quickly
buttons up again.

DEREK *sees everything.*

Then, fiddling in her bag, LYDIA *takes out a little syringe kit.
She loads a syringe from a little medical bottle. Then she injects
herself with the syringe. She does this quite briskly,
professionally.*

DEREK *is riveted.*

LYDIA *holds some cotton wool to her arm, then closes her
eyes. Then she gets up, clears away.*

DEREK *hides.*
She opens up the caravan door and steps out.
She stretches, like a dancer. Some steps.

At the mouth of the path she takes a moment to take in this world.

Then she walks down the track.

When she has gone, DEREK *goes closer to the caravan. He
takes the blooded handkerchief out of his notebook.*

*He looks at it, fearful, awestruck – like it has all the power in
the universe.*

Scene Six

Derek Knows

By the caravan. A grey morning.

DEREK *and* LYDIA.

DEREK	Thanks for coming
LYDIA	Sorry I
DEREK	Thank you.
LYDIA	(*A little briskly.*) I can't stay that long.
DEREK	Sure.
LYDIA	I'm sorry I didn't call.
DEREK	Don't worry about that.

LYDIA   It's been really busy.

DEREK   I know…
Finding your feet.

LYDIA   Yes.

Pause.

DEREK   Lydia… there's something I have to say to you.

Pause.

LYDIA   (*Getting the wrong end of the stick.*) Derek, I
think you're really / sweet

DEREK   No, you misunderstand / me.

LYDIA   Really, I think you're lovely, / but

DEREK   Please listen to / me.

LYDIA   I'm not sure / that.

DEREK   No, I understand.

LYDIA   I'm not really in a / place…

DEREK   That wasn't why…

Lydia, I want you to know that you can trust me.

Pause.

LYDIA   What are you talking about?

DEREK   I can help you, Lydia.

LYDIA   To what?

DEREK   If you need it.

LYDIA   I don't know what you mean.

DEREK   I was walking here last night.

And the…
The light was on. In the caravan.

Pause.

And I saw you.

Pause.

                   With the needle.

                   Pause.

                   There's a new shot, isn't there?

LYDIA   What do you mean?

DEREK   I read that they're trialling a new drug.

LYDIA   I don't know what you're talking about.

DEREK   And I saw the mark.

LYDIA   You were watching me?

DEREK   I was just *there*.

LYDIA   You were *watching me*?

DEREK   I was in the wrong / place.

LYDIA   You can't watch me!

DEREK   At the wrong time.

LYDIA   It's nothing!

DEREK   I'm so sorry.

LYDIA   (*Desperate.*) It's nothing! It wasn't that!

DEREK   My heart goes out to / you

LYDIA   No, no, no!

DEREK   If there's anything I can do.

LYDIA   You don't know what you're saying!

                   You don't *know*.

DEREK   Please.

LYDIA   Little fucking
                   Fucking nothing.
                   Creep.

                   She screws herself up, the ugliness of her anger.

                   Get away from me! Get away!

                   Beat.

He starts to stumble off, but she suddenly
struggles.
He hears.
He turns round.

LYDIA   (*Struggles.*) Oh shit.

She closes her eyes, feeling like she will faint.

DEREK *turns back.*

DEREK   Are you okay?

LYDIA   Just go!

Pause. DEREK *doesn't know what to do.*
She starts to crumple.

DEREK   Can I help you?

LYDIA   No.

DEREK   Please sit.

She sits.

It's okay.
It'll be okay.

Pause. DEREK *goes to give her a bottle of water*
from his bag.

She drinks it, without her lips touching the rim.

LYDIA   My lips haven't touched it.

DEREK   It's okay.

Pause. DEREK *tries to approach.*

LYDIA   Don't come close.

DEREK   Why not?

LYDIA   You could die.

DEREK   I won't die.

Pause.

LYDIA   Was it *obvious*?

DEREK	No.
LYDIA	It *isn't* obvious!
DEREK	I was in the wrong place at the wrong time.

Pause.

You don't have to be friends with me.
You don't have to see me.
But I just want you to know you can trust me.

I'll be your excuse, if you need one.

I'll be your lookout.

I won't ask for anything.

I won't breathe a word!

Pause. LYDIA looks at him. He smiles.

Pause. The sound of the sea.

It's high tide now.

Everything's washed away.
Forgotten.

LYDIA *suddenly struggles.*

It'll be okay, don't you worry.
You'll be as right as rain.

LYDIA *rallies.*

LYDIA   Do you have any food?

DEREK *runs inside the caravan and comes out with an apple and a chocolate bar.*

He hands her the apple, and then:

DEREK   Chocolate.

Pause. LYDIA eats.

Is it okay?

She's stronger now.

Are you feeling any better?

LYDIA   I can control it.
           With my shot
           If I'm lucky I might live for ages.
           I might live to be old.

           It doesn't matter at all on a day-to-day –
           (*Of whatever is inside her body*.) It doesn't
           wake up!
           It's sleeping.
           I ignore it.
           It doesn't concern me.

           You can't get it from just touching me.

           You could touch me now and you'd never get it.

           And not through
           Not through
           Kissing.

           The medication... suppresses it.
           I'm not contagious any more.
           And I'm so careful
           The idea of passing it / on

DEREK   You don't need / to

LYDIA   I want you to know that.

           Pause.

           I went... to the pub... with Vince.
           There was this guy.
           He was doing a speech.

           He was so clever.
           You could see his eyes dart around the room.
           Every time he looked at you:
           'Is he one?' 'Is she one?'
           He looked at me, and he knew.

DEREK   He couldn't.

LYDIA   I don't know how but he did.

           You saw my mark?

           It's horrible.

DEREK	No.

LYDIA   It's foul.

DEREK   It's just a mark.

Pause.

LYDIA   (*The nightmare looming again.*) I can't do it
again.

I can't.

Pause.

Last time, I had to move, when they found out.
In Sussex.

They found the house I was living in.
Bricks through the window.

Threats.
The poor people who were putting me up, they
had to leave, too.

DEREK   And your parents, are they?

LYDIA   No, they're not dead.

Pause.

I live with this woman now.
She's
They're in a kind of network.

DEREK   A network?

LYDIA   There are some people
Who want to help us.
Because there are places now where it's too
dangerous.
Attacks.
So the network help us move.

She's
She's really into it.
Political.
It's a bit much to be honest.

DEREK   I've heard
          I've heard there's this
          Woman.

LYDIA   No, it's just fairy stories.

DEREK   Right.

          They look out. Pause.

LYDIA   It's so quiet here.

          They listen to the silence.

          And the sea.
          Is this what you write about?

DEREK   Yes.

          And also characters.
          And things I'm feeling.

LYDIA   Can I read something?

DEREK   None of it's any good.

LYDIA   That doesn't matter.

DEREK   I wrote a story about a trawlerman that was okay.

          Pause.

          I think I have a copy of it somewhere.

          Pause. He rummages in his bag and then finds some typed pages.

          Please don't feel you have to.

LYDIA   You don't make me feel I have to do anything.

          Pause.

DEREK   I've been

          I've been meaning to ask

          What music do you like?

LYDIA   Loads of things.

DEREK   Yeah?

LYDIA	What do you like?
DEREK	Nineties.
LYDIA	Nineties?
DEREK	(*Smiling*.) Yeah.

She smiles.

I'll do you a tape.

LYDIA	A tape?
DEREK	Well, a CD.
LYDIA	Old-school!
DEREK	I'm not very good with new things

VINCENT *enters*.

VINCENT	Hi.
LYDIA	Hi.
VINCENT	I was looking for you.
LYDIA	Okay.
VINCENT	Come to the pub! It's packed. It's gonna be a *night*. They'll be singing later.

Are you coming?

Pause.

LYDIA	(*To* DEREK.) Do you want to come?

Pause.

DEREK	I don't think I should.
LYDIA	You should come.
DEREK	No... I won't. But you go.

Pause.

VINCENT	(*To* LYDIA.) Are you coming, then?

LYDIA   I don't think so.

VINCENT   I'll buy you a drink.

LYDIA   I'm alright.

VINCENT   You enjoyed yourself last time.

LYDIA   I need an early night.

VINCENT   Why?

LYDIA   I'm going swimming tomorrow.

               Beat.

               Do you want to come, Derek?

DEREK   Sure. What time?

LYDIA   When would be best?

DEREK   Tide's at eleven, so how about here at ten-thirty?

LYDIA   Perfect.

               Pause.

DEREK   I'll see you tomorrow, then!

LYDIA   Yes.

               Pause. She exits.

               Pause. VINCENT *looks on.*

VINCENT   Just be careful, mate.

DEREK   Eh?

VINCENT   I don't want you to get hurt.
               I don't want you to think 'oh things are going
               pretty well for me' when they're not.

               Is that what you think?
               'I'm quietly confident.'
               This new girl with the sweetest breath in
               England, she turns up and for some reason, for a
               few moments, she's showing you some interest.

               It's a mistake, Derek.
               It's a mistake that awkward shy boys have made
               throughout history.

When everything is up in the air, when
everything's new, this kind of girl they can
sometimes make mistakes. Jumble people up.
Get trapped with the wrong company.

And the longer they're trapped the more vicious
the snap will be.

DEREK   What you on about?

VINCENT   Your goodness won't turn her on.
It'll just make her feel terrible.

Pause.

I'm going to fuck her, Derek.
I just know it. It's like destiny.
I will.
I'll fuck her and there'll be fireworks all over
London.
That's what I'm going to do.

DEREK   You won't.

VINCENT   Why not?

DEREK   You just won't

VINCENT   Why not?

DEREK   Leave it.

VINCENT   Of course, I know there must be some 'thing'
about her.
There's always some 'thing' about girls like her.
With a reason to be shy.
Is she the girl who gets addicted?
Or doesn't like to eat.
Or hides the cuts on her arms?

I don't care.
I don't care about any of that stuff.

Pause.

Are we still friends, Derek?

DEREK   Yes.

VINCENT   Do you promise?

DEREK   Yes.

VINCENT   I wish my soul could be more like yours.

           VINCENT *gets out his knife*.

           Do you trust me?

DEREK   Yes.

VINCENT   I want to prove to you that I care for you.

           How can I prove it?

DEREK   You don't need to prove it.

           VINCENT *cuts his own hand with his knife*.

           No, Vince.

VINCENT   Do you think I'm a good person?

DEREK   I do.

           VINCENT *holds* DEREK*'s hand*.

VINCENT   Will you always be my friend?

DEREK   Yes.

VINCENT   Are we blood brothers?

           Pause.

           Don't worry, the knife's sharp.

           VINCENT *cuts* DEREK*'s arm*. DEREK *cries out*.

           That wasn't so bad, was it?

           VINCENT *puts his bleeding hand on* DEREK*'s arm*.

           That wasn't so bad.

           DEREK *struggles with feelings of fainting*.

           What's wrong with you?

           Are you alright?

DEREK   Yes.

VINCENT	Don't faint.
DEREK	I'm not.
VINCENT	It was nothing. You haven't gone through anything.
DEREK	No.
VINCENT	You've no right to be all frightened.
DEREK	No.
VINCENT	You're always fucking frightened, but I'm not that bad. I could make you lost again, but I'm not that bad. You've never really been through anything really shit, Derek. I'm sorry, but you haven't.

Scene Seven

A Swim

By the caravan. A lovely bright day, a bit of a breeze.

DEREK *runs in quickly from the beach, up the path barefoot, trying not to run on anything sharp. He is wearing faded old swimming shorts, a bit big.*

He looks back to the sea as he dries himself off with a towel.

LYDIA *runs in, in a one-piece swimming suit. She dries herself with her towel.*

DEREK	Alright?
LYDIA	Yes!
DEREK	Nippy breeze!
	DEREK *dries himself with his towel, then puts it around his shoulders.*
LYDIA	How was that!

DEREK   Wonderful!

               LYDIA *closes her eyes and feels something.*

LYDIA   I love this bit.
               After swimming.
               The tingling feeling.

               Do you get that?

DEREK   Yes.

               *She picks up her clothes, and goes into the
               caravan.*

LYDIA   I'm getting changed.

DEREK   Okay.

               *She opens the window, wide, and pokes her
               head out.*

LYDIA   Is there anyone coming?

DEREK   No.

               DEREK *turns around as she gets changed in the
               caravan, and remains loyally disinterested in
               what is going on behind him.*

               LYDIA *takes off her swimsuit. She quickly puts
               on some knickers and jeans. Shielding her chest
               with her arm, she briefly looks up to see if*
               DEREK *is watching.*

               They are both aware of what might be there.

LYDIA   I don't want you to see it.

               Beat.

               It's horrible.

DEREK   It is what it is.

LYDIA   It's like evil.

DEREK   It's not evil.

               Maybe it will fade.

LYDIA   And scar.

DEREK   We all get scars.

             Pause. LYDIA *looks at* DEREK, *then finishes
             getting dressed, comes out of the caravan.*

             DEREK *goes into the caravan, and brings out a
             CD he has made.*

             I made you a CD!

LYDIA   Oh!

             Pause. He hands it to her.

DEREK   I'm going to get changed now.

LYDIA   I'll turn round.

LYDIA   (*Of the inlay card, upon which is neatly written
             the name of each track.*) You wrote it all out!

DEREK   Yes!

LYDIA   You made me a CD!

DEREK   Yes.

LYDIA   Shall we play it?

DEREK   Alright.
             I'll bring the thing out here.

             DEREK *finishes changing, and then drags his
             CD player out of the caravan, which is connected
             to an extension cable.*

             He puts the CD in, and presses play.

             A song begins, from 1995. It is a wonderful song.

LYDIA   Who's this?

DEREK   Oh

             He hands the CD case to LYDIA. *She looks.*

LYDIA   I don't know it.

             When did it come out?

DEREK   1995.

Pause. They listen to the song for a bit. What a wonderful song.

I don't think we have to fall into the abyss, you know?

I think we can all find a way through.
There's no reason why we can't.

Don't you think?

I remember
When it was on the news for the first time.
When all those people started dying in London.
In London!
So many people, in our country!
And we started getting very frightened.
And the blaming began:
'This is so typical.'
'These city people with their loose…'
'Well, this is what happens when you behave like that.'

Pause.

If we had stood up for your people

LYDIA   I don't have a people.
          We're not a 'people'.

DEREK   You're brave.

LYDIA   I'm not brave.

DEREK   (*Bravely putting his hand on her shoulder.*) You are. I've seen it.

          But that hand on her is the last straw, she snaps.

LYDIA   Get your hand off me.

          Beat.

DEREK   I think you have such courage.

LYDIA   Then you don't know me.

DEREK   I think you're a good person.

LYDIA   How do you think I got it?

               Pause. LYDIA *starts to anger.*

               Don't make me feel bad.

DEREK   I'm sorry.

LYDIA   You're making me feel shit.

DEREK   I'm so sorry

LYDIA   And you've got one over me.

DEREK   I'd never say *anything*!

               VINCENT *enters.*

VINCENT   Never say what?

               He is carrying a bunch of wildflowers.

               Hello.

LYDIA   Hello.

VINCENT   (*Of the flowers.*) I brought you these.

               These are poppies.
               And bugle.
               And dog roses.
               And elderflower.
               Honeysuckle.
               Ragged Robin.

LYDIA   How do you know all their names?

VINCENT   My mum used to teach me.
               She used to have a florist.

               They're showing a film at the hall tonight.

LYDIA   What is it?

VINCENT   *Four Weddings and a Funeral*
               Have you seen it?

LYDIA   Yeah.

VINCENT   We could go for a drink, afterwards.

               Pause.

LYDIA   I'd like that.

           Pause.

VINCENT   Do you want to come, Del?

DEREK   I need to get home.

LYDIA   Yeah.

DEREK   Do the supper.

LYDIA   Yeah.

           Beat. DEREK *exits down the track.*

VINCENT   What's wrong with him?

           VINCENT *has a bottle of beer. He offers it to her.*

LYDIA   No thanks.

           VINCENT *takes the top off the bottle of beer.*

VINCENT   Go on, take it.

           LYDIA *takes it. She watches him.*

LYDIA   Have you got one for yourself?

           Pause. VINCENT *pulls out another beer.
           Relieved she won't have to share a bottle, she
           takes a sip.*

VINCENT   Have I done something wrong, Lydia?

LYDIA   No.

VINCENT   I thought there was something going on
           between us?

           Pause.

           Was I wrong about that?

           Pause.

           I haven't been very happy recently.

           I've been feeling very angry.
           A black dog inside.

           I really like you, you know.

I can't stop thinking about you.
I think about you constantly.

Pause. He tries to gently touch her, but she pushes him off.

LYDIA   (*Gently.*) No.

VINCENT   Come on.

LYDIA   I'm sorry.

VINCENT   What's wrong with me?

LYDIA   There's nothing wrong with you.

             PETER *enters, with his briefcase, via the path.*

VINCENT   What are you doing?

PETER   I'm sorry.

VINCENT   Spying on us!

PETER   I was just passing.
             I didn't mean any interruption.

             (*To* LYDIA.) Sorry, darling.
             Sorry.
             I've seen you before, haven't I?
             You came to my talk?

LYDIA   Yes.

PETER   I hope it wasn't too boring.

LYDIA   No.

PETER   What did you think, love?

LYDIA   Yeah, it was good.

PETER   Or did you think I was just speaking a load of
             bollocks?

LYDIA   (*Looking down, ashamed.*) No.

PETER   That's fine if you did.
             It's a free country!

             Pause.

I just try and stay honest.
We're fighting to stay alive, here!

Pause.

We're fighting for a future!
Ain't that right?

What's your name?

Pause. He looks at her, eyes glittering!

LYDIA   Lydia.

PETER   Where do you live, Lydia?

LYDIA   I don't give out my address.

PETER   Okay, fair play.

Do you know about the sickness in this land,
Lydia?
Do you know why this is happening to us?
Do you know why?

Pause.

This is punishment for the way they were living.
And the parents

VINCENT   You speak such a load of rubbish, you know.

PETER   Yeah?

VINCENT   I heard your speech.
It was rubbish.

The things you say, they aren't right.
You just speak a load of lies, you know.

Pause. VINCENT *gets up, squares up to* PETER.

Who the hell are you? Coming here from
wherever you are, with your briefcase?

PETER   Okay.

VINCENT   Talking bollocks.

PETER   Okay, boy.
               That's okay.
               It's good. That you've got feelings.
               Why don't we talk about it?

VINCENT   I'm just trying to get drunk, here.
               I'm trying to get to know this lady.
               It's a Saturday night.
               I don't want to talk about nothing with some old
               fucker in a leather jacket!

               Pause. PETER considers all manner of things.

PETER   (*To* VINCENT.) Okay.
               Okay, let's leave it.

               Pause.

               You enjoy yourself tonight.

               You enjoy yourself.

               Just so long as you know...
               That these days – days like this – glorious days –
               these days are numbered.
               Nights like this are numbered.
               When there's sweetness in the air and
               wildflowers.
               You cherish these nights.

               Pause. PETER exits.

               VINCENT *and* LYDIA *burst out laughing as he
               walks up the track.*

Scene Eight

Drunk

That night. By the caravan. The light of the moon.

LYDIA *and* VINCENT *run in, joyously drunk. They stop.*

VINCENT   Here we are.

                     VINCENT *offers* LYDIA *a little bottle of vodka.*

                     Finish it.

LYDIA   No, I'm gone.

VINCENT   Yeah?

LYDIA   I'm really gone.

VINCENT   Did you have a good time?

LYDIA   (*Coyly.*) It was fine.

VINCENT   Fine?

LYDIA   (*Smiling.*) It was fine.

                     I haven't got this fucked in ages.

                     Pause.

VINCENT   When were you last this fucked?

                     *They smile. Pause. They become aware of their
                     surroundings.*

                     Do you think he's here?

LYDIA   (*Laughing.*) Shhhhhhhhhh!

VINCENT   Derek, are you in here?

LYDIA   Shhhhhhh!

VINCENT   You're good at dancing.

LYDIA   Thank you.

VINCENT   It was a good night.

LYDIA   Did you like the music?

VINCENT   You know what I'd really like?

LYDIA   What?

           VINCENT *indicates the caravan.*

VINCENT   Get you in there.

LYDIA   (*Mock outrage.*) I'm not going in there!

           VINCENT *goes into the caravan.*

           I'm not!

           VINCENT *re-emerges, with* DEREK*'s notebook.*

VINCENT   Look at this.

LYDIA   What have you got?

VINCENT   (*Reading by the light of the moon.*) 'You are
           okay'

LYDIA   Is / that – [DEREK*'s notebook*]?

VINCENT   'One day you / will'

LYDIA   Don't read it!

VINCENT   'One day you will grow your wings.'
           (*Impersonating* DEREK.) 'These are just a few
           notes, Lydia.'

LYDIA   Don't read it!

VINCENT   'One day she came out of the sea.'

LYDIA   Stop it!

VINCENT   'She crawled out of the mud, quietly.
           Shy and beautiful
           Brushing off sand and / shells.

LYDIA   No, seriously

VINCENT   And over marsh and pool she looked straight into
           my eyes.
           And even from that distance he knew she could
           understand him.
           And knew she had the answers.
           To all the things that hurt or didn't make sense.'

           Pause.

                (Turning to LYDIA.) Do you think this bit is
                about you, Lydia?

LYDIA   No!

VINCENT   Do you find it rather beautiful?

LYDIA   No!

VINCENT   But do you think it is 'good writing'?

                LYDIA *smiles.*

                He flushes when he sees you.

LYDIA   Does he?

VINCENT   Do I flush too?

LYDIA   When you've had a few pints.

VINCENT   That's okay.

                VINCENT *smiles. He goes in for the kiss, but she*
                pulls back.

LYDIA   No, not yet.

                She holds his head in place with her hand. She
                kisses him on the cheek.

                He kisses her on the cheek.

                They enjoy the moment.

VINCENT   (*Shouting out loud, to the sky.*) Derek, are you
                watching?
                Because if you're watching could you stop
                watching, now?

                She smiles. He kisses her neck. She looks down,
                suddenly invaded with dread.

                (*Joking.*) I bet you do this with Derek, too?

LYDIA   (*Outraged.*) No!
                I wouldn't.

VINCENT   Why not?

LYDIA   I couldn't go with someone like him.

               He's nothing, he's just

               Pause.

               There is some scuffling in the grasses. As if someone were running away.

               What was that?

VINCENT   What?

LYDIA   Like there was something in the bushes.

VINCENT   Probably a fox.

LYDIA   Oh shit.
               Do you think it was him?

VINCENT   No.

               Pause.

               He leans in to kiss her, but the thought has possessed her.

               Are you okay?

LYDIA   Yes.

VINCENT   What?

               What did I do?

               She pulls away.

               What did I do?

               She pulls away.

               What's wrong?

Scene Nine

Persuasion

DEREK *sits on the step of the caravan. A hot hot day.*

PETER *enters.*

PETER Hello, boy.

   What's wrong?

   What's wrong, buddy?

   Who is it?

   Has something happened?

DEREK (*Angrily.*) No.

PETER It's alright!

DEREK Please go away.

PETER What's happened, mate?

   Don't be frightened.

   I'm just trying to help you.

   Pause.

   Why do you hate me?

DEREK I don't.

PETER There's too much hate in this world isn't there?

   The only thing I hate is hatred, Derek.

   Pause. He looks about.

   It's not right, is it, that a boy like you, a good boy,
   a really good boy, should have to grow up like this.
   I grew up when there was some hope in the world.
   And now look what's happening.

   Pause.

   You thinking about her?

   That girl you're sweet on.

DEREK   I'm not sweet on / her

PETER   Course you are.

           You know they went off together?

           You know they went off together last night?

           We all saw them leave the pub?
           His hand on her arse.

           Pause.

           Where does she live?

DEREK   I don't know.

PETER   Exactly.

DEREK   (*Pointing.*) Over that way.

PETER   Who lives down there, though?

           Pause.

           It's just puzzling isn't it?
           How we never see where she goes.

           Women, eh?
           They make you feel good for a minute, and that
           minute it feels so good, doesn't it?

           Do you know what I mean, Derek?
           When you feel you have a trust?
           She makes you feel special. For a few moments.
           Just for a few moment.

           And then something snaps, you don't know why,
           but it snaps, it's unexplainable.
           And it's all gone.

           I'm through with women now.
           I just serve the Lord.

           Pause.

           She's clever, isn't she?

           The way she pulled you in.

And now you're feeling lost, and confused.
But don't worry. That feeling will go away.
Because there's a greater love, isn't there?

There's a love that won't let you down.
God… and country.
Because you love this country, I know that.

Derek, I've got a pal who's a whizz with a
computer.
And he hacked into a list from the district
hospital.

There are three type-thirty-seven contaminants
registered for the trial drug in this borough alone,
as of two weeks ago.
Of course, they deny it / when

DEREK   It's not her.

PETER   No?

DEREK   It's not her.

PETER   It's okay.

DEREK   It isn't.

PETER   We're not interested in causing trouble.

DEREK   It's not her.

PETER   I just want you to be careful.

          Pause.

          Are you not afraid you'll catch it?

DEREK   No.

PETER   It doesn't work you know.
          The suppressant.
          How could it work?
          This thing, there isn't an earthly cure.
          This is real, you know
          This isn't a story.

          Look.

          He hands DEREK *some pictures.*

DEREK *looks away, disgusted.*

VINCENT *enters.*

Alright, Vince!

VINCENT   I'm good, yeah.

PETER   You look perky!

VINCENT   Oh my goodness I had a night.

PETER   Did you?

VINCENT   It's on, Derek.

DEREK   Yeah?

VINCENT   It's on.

Pause.

We came back here.

PETER   Yeah?

VINCENT   It keeps coming back to me.

PETER   You see it through, boy?

VINCENT   Next time.

PETER   How far did you go?

VINCENT   She wants to take things slow.

PETER   Does she? That's interesting.

VINCENT   She's not any old slut, but I'll get in there, make no mistake.

PETER   You're going to sink yourself in?

VINCENT   (*Savouring a memory.*) Oh my god.

PETER   You've arranged another date?

VINCENT   She's coming here.

PETER   When?

VINCENT   I think I might love her, you know?

PETER   What do think, Derek?

             Shall we tell him?

VINCENT   What?

PETER   Shall we tell him, Del?

VINCENT   Tell me what?

DEREK   There's nothing to tell.

PETER   Go on.

DEREK   It's nothing.

VINCENT   Derek, what is it?

             Pause.

PETER   (*To* DEREK.) You're a good kid, trying to protect
             her, but you can't keep your secret any more.
             Cos now she's putting Vince at risk.

VINCENT   What is it?

PETER   Tell him, Derek.

VINCENT   Tell me what?

PETER   This is life or death.

             Tell him what's in your heart.

VINCENT   I know what's in his heart.
             I know he fancies her.
             But he can't have her.

             Cos she thinks you're really weird, Derek.
             She thinks you're a creep.
             We were laughing about you.

             The things she was doing I know she wants it!
             Do you know what we're going to do?

DEREK   You can't.

VINCENT   No?

DEREK   You can't.

PETER   Why not?

VINCENT   Why can't I?

DEREK   You can't.

PETER   Good lad.

VINCENT   Why?

PETER   Tell him.

DEREK   I saw her take a shot.

VINCENT   What do you mean?

            Pause.

PETER   Good boy.

DEREK   She's one of them.

            Pause. He is suddenly full of disgust.

            She's got it.

            There's a mark on her.
            This horrible mark.

PETER   (*To* DEREK.) You'll be rewarded for this.

VINCENT   (*Still coming to terms.*) She's…

PETER   She's done you for a mug, Vincent, this is classic,
            this is, this is a classic trick.
            So tell us what you did and maybe it's not too late.

            Pause. LYDIA *arrives. The males don't say
            anything.*

LYDIA   Hi.

            Pause. They stare at her.

            What's wrong?

            Pause.

DEREK   Oh god.

LYDIA   What?

VINCENT   Don't come close.

DEREK   Oh no.

LYDIA   What's going on?

She puts a hand on VINCENT*'s arm.* VINCENT *whips it off.*

VINCENT   Don't touch me

LYDIA   What?

VINCENT   Don't touch me!

DEREK   Vince, please, / drop it.

LYDIA   What is it?

DEREK   I didn't mean / to

VINCENT   On first glance you look pretty good but if you look hard you / can see

LYDIA   What are you talking about?

VINCENT   I can't believe I was taken in.

LYDIA   By what?

VINCENT   Your foul blood, Derek's told us all about you.

LYDIA   What did you say?

VINCENT   Oh my lord the thought that you were wet / for me.

LYDIA   It's not true!

VINCENT   The slime dripping down your leg was meant for me.

He works himself up.

I thought you
I thought you

She appeals to him, coming close to him.

Don't come close to me!

LYDIA	Derek!
	DEREK *looks down*.
	Derek, tell him you made it up.
DEREK	I made it up.
LYDIA	Tell him!
VINCENT	(*To* LYDIA.) Is that why you came here? 'On your holidays.' You thought you could hide here?
	Poisoning the water supply, dripping blood.
LYDIA	I / don't
VINCENT	Don't tell me what you do or don't. Just you is enough.
DEREK	Vince.
VINCENT	We don't want you here.
DEREK	Stop it.
	VINCENT *hurtles towards* LYDIA *but* PETER *gets in the way*.
PETER	(*To* DEREK.) It's alright, boy.
VINCENT	(*To* LYDIA.) You'll probably die tomorrow.
PETER	Hold on, mate.
VINCENT	(*To* LYDIA.) I'm not finished with you!
	LYDIA *turns to* DEREK.
LYDIA	How could you?
	DEREK *closes his eyes*.
	(*To* DEREK.) I thought you were with me.
	DEREK *doesn't know what to say*.
	I thought I could trust you.
PETER	Oi!
	DEREK *struggles*.

LYDIA   (*To* DEREK.) Fuck off, you little shit, just fuck off.

PETER   Don't you speak to him like that.

LYDIA   (*To* DEREK.) Get away from me.
             You nasty thing.
             Get away!

             DEREK *runs away.*

             Pause.
             LYDIA *turns to face the other two. Suddenly
             realising the situation she is in.*

             It's alright, I'm going.

             PETER *begins to put on some surgical gloves.*

             You won't see me again.

             PETER *throws* VINCENT *some of the gloves.*

PETER   Oh no, we're not finished with you yet.

             Vince, put these on.

             PETER *gets out his phone, and makes a call.*

             (*Into the phone.*) Yeah, we've sniffed her out.

             PETER *approaches* LYDIA, *who retreats,
             terrified. She backs against the caravan.*

             (*Into phone.*) Yeah, we're going to give her the
             warning.

Scene Ten

A Meditation

In the darkness, a recording: the voice of the OLD LADY.
A meditation.

OLD LADY I've got my heart.
       I've got my heart.
       I've got my blood.
       I've got my blood.
       I've got my wings.
       I've seen the way.

       I'm going to be born.
       I'm going to be born any day.

       Any day this search will be over.
       Any day I'll find you.
       And take you home.

Scene Eleven

The Blood

*By the caravan, half an hour later. The sky is now half-overcast
and reddish, as if bloodshot.*

LYDIA *lies against the caravan, covered in blood, only half-
conscious.* DEREK *is by her.*

DEREK   What happened?

      LYDIA *cries out.*

      Why?
      What did they do this for?

      LYDIA *cries out.*

      I need to get a doctor.

LYDIA   No!

DEREK   I'm going to get you home.

            He goes to hold her, ready to pick her up.

LYDIA   Don't touch me!

            DEREK *releases her.*

            My blood!

            Pause. He has blood all over him. He looks at his bloody hands, unsure of them.

DEREK   It's alright.

LYDIA   You can't touch it!

            DEREK *looks up the track.*

DEREK   There's someone coming, we've got to get you away

LYDIA   No, I can't I can't.

            He watches the person enter, from the track, on an old bicycle.

            It is SARAH, LYDIA*'s guardian. She has dismounted onto one pedal before the bicycle has even stopped.*

SARAH   Oh my darling.

            She assesses LYDIA *quickly – her pulse, etc.*

DEREK   She was attacked.

SARAH   Yes.

DEREK   I think it's the League.

SARAH   There's been chatter online.

            (*To* DEREK.) You can help me.

            SARAH *lifts up her bike. It has a pannier rack.* SARAH *gets on again.*

            (*To* DEREK.) Lift her onto it.

            Pause.

            Come on, quickly.

DEREK	Are you sure?
SARAH	Is your skin broken?
DEREK	No.
SARAH	You've not ingested any?
DEREK	No.
SARAH	So help lift her up, you can wash yourself later.

DEREK lifts LYDIA onto the pannier rack.

DEREK	Where are we taking her?
SARAH	*(Ignoring him, and turning to LYDIA.)* Lydia, put your arms around me.
DEREK	I want to help
SARAH	If you want to help her you'll stay away and keep quiet. Do not identify me Do not go to the police. Do not say a word.
DEREK	I won't say anything.
SARAH	Somebody has. Somebody has betrayed her.
DEREK	Is she going to be okay?
SARAH	She will be saved.
DEREK	What do you mean?

SARAH cycles off, a little heavily, with the extra weight.

| SARAH | One way or the other, she'll be saved. |

Beat. DEREK runs after her but realises it is hopeless.

| DEREK | Lydia! |
| | Lydia! |

He looks at his hands, covered in blood. He holds
them there for some time, looking at them, the
horror of the blood, and feeling the panic build
inside him.

ACT TWO

Scene One

The Cottage

The next day.

An immaculate, blindingly whitewashed cottage near the sea.
High brambles surround a lovely English country garden.

A long driveway leads to a private road beyond.
Sunloungers, a jug of ice water on a table.

The sky is a deep vivid blue today and the sun is hot.

LYDIA *lies on one of the loungers. She is pale and bruised.*
Clean now, but groggy.

SARAH *enters.*

She busies herself checking LYDIA*'s pulse.*

She takes LYDIA*'s temperature, enters something on a*
clipboard.

LYDIA *stirs. Moans.*

She takes LYDIA*'s hand.*

SARAH   Look – the sun's out.
              That's good.
              The sun's a good healer.

              It's over now, darling.
              It's all over.

              You don't need to worry any more.

              We'll get you out of here.

              Find you somewhere else.

              SARAH *goes to kiss* LYDIA *on the head.*

Lydia, you are not alone.

You are not alone.

LYDIA *moans*.

It's over now.

It's alright.

LYDIA *cries out*.

These stupid people.

They don't understand how special you are.

They don't understand that your time is yet to come.

They don't understand that you too have a story.

Yes, you have a story.
And you will tell it.

Of how you lived.
And who you were.

LYDIA   You don't know what I did.

SARAH   Tell me.

LYDIA   No.

SARAH   You have a story.
And when you start to tell it.
You start to be reborn.

LYDIA   I don't want to be reborn.

SARAH   She's going to find you, you know.

She's going to find you.

LYDIA   Who?

SARAH   You know who.

LYDIA *isn't interested*.

She'll come.

Any day now, she'll come.

And she'll take you home.

Pause. There's a noise.

SARAH *hears it, looks up, suddenly full of attention.*

Who's there?

Who comes?

SARAH *moves up the track, away from* LYDIA.

DEREK *enters, wearing a baseball cap and sunglasses, as if he is in disguise. He is confused, agitated, exhausted.*

(*Imagining* DEREK *to be an intruder.*) No!

DEREK   It's okay!

It's me.

Derek.
I was
I was there!

SARAH   How did you find us?

DEREK   I don't know.
I just walked.

SARAH   You can't be here.

DEREK   I just had to find you.

SARAH   It's over now.

DEREK   How is she?

SARAH   She's in a bad way.

DEREK   Can I speak to her?

SARAH   She's with her own people, now.

DEREK   Her own people?

SARAH   She's not one of yours.

DEREK I don't have a people.
       I don't have anything against your / people.

SARAH (*With contempt*.) Looking around to see if anyone
       has spotted you. In your hat, and your sunglasses.
       Your disguise.

DEREK I burn easy.

SARAH You do not *know* heat.

DEREK I was just

SARAH There are plenty of you with 'justs' and good
       intentions.
       But you don't *know*.

LYDIA (*Who has not seen* DEREK *yet*.) Who is it?

DEREK (*Moving towards her*.) Lydia?

SARAH (*Moving to stop him*.) Boy.

       DEREK *heads for* LYDIA, *but* SARAH *gets in
       the way*.

DEREK Lydia.

LYDIA Derek?

       SARAH *tries to escort him away from her, but*
       DEREK *dodges her. He catches* LYDIA's *gaze*.
       Pause.

DEREK Please.

SARAH You must go now.

DEREK Lydia, I'm

SARAH She's too weak.

LYDIA Derek, what the fuck?

SARAH You're not well.

LYDIA (*To* DEREK.) Why have you come?

       Pause.

DEREK I needed to know you're alright.

LYDIA   Yeah?

DEREK   I'm so sorry.
I'm so sorry.

I can't stop / thinking

LYDIA   No?

DEREK   About why this has / happened.

LYDIA   No I bet you can't.

SARAH   (*To* LYDIA.) Don't excite yourself.

DEREK   And how shameful I am.

LYDIA   Don't worry about it.

DEREK   How awful.

LYDIA   I'm glad you are.
(*To* DEREK.) I'm glad you're weak
And ugly and nasty.
I'm glad you're a coward.

Pause.

DEREK   Yes.

SARAH   (*To* DEREK.) You must go now.

LYDIA   Let him stay.

SARAH   It's time for your shot.

LYDIA   (*With force.*) Let him stay.

SARAH   As your carer I can't allow it.

LYDIA   Let him stay!

She struggles with the exertion of this.

Pause. SARAH *accepts.*

SARAH   I'm going to prepare her dose.
I'll be a minute.
And then you must leave.

Pause. DEREK *nods.*

LYDIA   Why have you come?

DEREK   I told you.

LYDIA   No, that's not all.
           What else?
           What else is on your mind?
           There's something else.

           Pause.

           Something's happened.

           Pause.

DEREK   It's just

           When
           Afterwards

           There was blood on my hands.
           Your blood, and

LYDIA   Were your hands cut?

DEREK   No.

LYDIA   Did you wash them?

DEREK   Yes.

           But
           It was like
           At that moment.
           I knew something had changed.

           Inside me.
           Something was born.
           Something
           Something wrong.

           He closes his eyes.

           And I thought… what if I have it?

LYDIA   Derek, you idiot.

DEREK   Maybe I've always had it.

LYDIA   You idiot.

DEREK   I've always known it.

LYDIA   Derek, it's real.

DEREK   I know.

LYDIA   It's a real thing, it's not

           Look.

           *Pause. She gets herself up. She unbuttons her
           blouse. Pause. He looks at the mark, fearfully.*

           Look.

           Look at me!

           Look at the death all over me.
           It's real.
           It's inside me.
           It's black and sticky
           It's ice.
           It's boiling.
           It's hard.
           It's an oil slick.
           It's real.

           I can see it if I close my eyes.
           I try to pin it down but I can't.
           It drives me mad.

           You think you're like me?

           You think you're like me?

           Pause.

           *She reaches out for him. Her hand, slowly, to his
           head.*

           She moves to kiss him. He flinches.

           LYDIA *cries out.*

DEREK   Sorry.

           She starts to struggle.

           I'm so sorry.

           LYDIA *struggles.*

(*Shouting for* SARAH.) Miss!
Miss!

LYDIA *begins to faint.*
SARAH *emerges, rushing into action, feeling*
LYDIA*'s forehead.*

SARAH   Help me get her lying down.

DEREK *gently lays* LYDIA *down, her head
resting on his chest.* SARAH *gives* LYDIA *a
glass of water.*

LYDIA *is profusely sick – on herself and on*
DEREK.

SARAH *goes back inside.* DEREK *stares at*
LYDIA.

SARAH *quickly returns with a syringe that she
injects in* LYDIA*'s arm.*

Pause. DEREK *gets up. He walks away from the
cottage.*

Where are you going?

DEREK   I need to get this [*sick*] off.

SARAH   You can clean up inside.

DEREK *closes his eyes in a panic.*

I could do with your help.

DEREK   Sorry

SARAH   Derek

DEREK   I didn't realise the mark was so awful.

LYDIA   Derek, wait

DEREK   (*Panicking.*) I'm sorry, I can't

DEREK *hesitates.*

I'm so sorry.

He trips off quickly, before starting to run.

Scene Two

Beware Them Beware Them

PETER *preaches to his followers*.

PETER   Beware them, beware them, for they are coming!
                These creatures, we talk of smoking rabbits out
                of holes
                But what poisons run in their blood if they
                bite you?
                These creatures who dare not speak their real
                names
                Who mask their contamination.
                They look like you or I, unless you're looking
                Unless you know the signs and they betray a
                look, a slip, a naked arm.
                And in His light we will find them. And we will
                root them out.

                Beware of footpaths and what may lie in wait.
                Of handsome youngsters too easy to smile.
                Beware lazy bearded men who say they love
                to hike
                Who say 'oh, it could never happen here'.
                Who invite you to their cottage in the woods.
                An innocent remark about a fire and teacakes.
                When you're in it's too late.

                Beware them for they are coming!
                And when the time comes we must be ready.
                When they make their move we must be ready.
                When the time comes we will be ready.
                And in His light we will find them. And we will
                root them out.

Scene Three

Conspirators

By the caravan. A week later.
Towards the end of the day. DEREK *sits on top of the caravan looking at the sea.*

VINCENT *enters.* DEREK *starts, turns round – it looks like he hasn't slept for days.*

VINCENT   It's alright.
            It's me.

            I've come here every day hoping you'd be back.

            Are you alright?

DEREK   Yeah.

VINCENT   Where have you been?

            Everyone's been looking for you.

            It's a lovely evening.

            We could go to the pools, like we used to.

            Look for tiddlers.

            Pause. DEREK *turns back to look at the sea.*

            I was thinking, this morning
            About that time you found that cormorant with
            the broken wing.

            And you tried to help it.

DEREK   I should never have done that.

VINCENT   It was kind.

DEREK   It died.

VINCENT   I always felt a better person after I'd been with
            you.

            Pause.

            There's a group of us.
            Young people.
            With the League.

We're going to do all kinds of things
Start something positive!
Community things!
Clean things up!

Pause.

I miss you, Derek.
I wish I saw more of you.

Peter wants to see you, too.
He really esteems you.
He wants to be a father to you like he's a father
to me.

Old friend?
Will you see him?
Please?
He's asked me.

Pause. DEREK turns round, and nods. VINCENT goes off, and gives the signal to PETER, who enters, carrying a four-pack of lager.

PETER   I just wanna start by saying thank you, Derek.
Thank you for agreeing to meet me.
Thank you from the bottom of my heart.

(*Of the sea.*) It's beautiful isn't it?

This is where the battle's being fought, Derek.
This is what we're fighting for.

DEREK *looks away.*

I can see you're a really good kid.
A nice kid.
You've never deserved this.
This was other people. Not you.
It's not your fault this happened.

We should get you some new clothes.

PETER *indicates* VINCENT*'s shirt.*

Look at this shirt!

I got Vince this shirt, it's nice, isn't it?

DEREK   Yeah.

PETER   Would you like a shirt like that?

DEREK   Maybe.

PETER   Go on, Vince.

Beat. VINCENT *doesn't understand.*

Take it off.

VINCENT   Eh?

PETER   Take off your shirt.

DEREK   No, it's / alright.

PETER   (*To* VINCENT.) Go on, you can swap.
You got plenty of shirts, Vince!

DEREK   It's alright, Peter.

PETER   Vincent.

VINCENT   It's new!

PETER   (*To* VINCENT.) What have I talked about?
Loving kindness? Eh?

Pause. VINCENT *takes off his shirt.*

(*To* DEREK, *still on top of the caravan*.) Come
on, get down.

DEREK *climbs down.*
VINCENT *gives the shirt to* DEREK.
VINCENT*'s torso is clear of marks.*

(*Of* VINCENT*'s body.*) Look at that good clean
English trunk!

(*To* DEREK, *of the shirt.*) Go on, try it on.

DEREK   What, here?

PETER   We're all men of the world, Derek.

Pause.

What's the problem, Derek?

Pause.

DEREK   I don't want to take his shirt, Peter.

PETER   (*Approvingly, of* DEREK.) You learn from this
           kid, Vincent.

VINCENT   Yeah.

PETER   Loving kindness.

           Pause.

           (*To* DEREK.) Go on, son.
           Go on. Try on the shirt.
           Let's see you.

           Pause. DEREK *closes his eyes. He slowly takes
           his shirt off, as if he doesn't know what will be
           underneath. There are no marks.*

           Look at that!

           Good clean English trunk.

           DEREK *puts* VINCENT'*s shirt on.*

           It looks good, that does!

DEREK   Yeah?

PETER   Wonderful.

PETER   Do you want a beer, Derek?

DEREK   No, I'm alright.

PETER   Have a beer, mate, go on.

           PETER *takes a beer and gives it to* DEREK.
           DEREK *tastes the beer, and doesn't much like it.*

           How do you like it?

DEREK   I don't much like beer.

PETER   Bit bitter?

DEREK   Yeah.

PETER   We should have started you on cider.

           DEREK *takes another sip.*

           That's right. Keep going, you'll get a taste for it.

You are a man, you know.
You have been growing.
I've seen it.

I've seen you become a man in these last weeks.

I just want you to know that any information you
have, it's all safe, we're not going to do anything.

DEREK   I don't know anything.

PETER   Sure.

DEREK   I don't want another attack.

PETER   That's not what we're about, Derek.
We don't want violence.
Now, if you wanna talk to 'em, be friends with
'em, that's your prerogative, it's a free country.

DEREK   I don't

PETER   But honestly
Be careful, brother.

It breaks my heart to see a clever kid like you in
a pickle.
Cos you are in a pickle aren't you?

I know you're worried about her. But that's good.
It shows you have a heart.

(*Approvingly*.) Derek, you've got a heart in you.
(*To* VINCENT.) He cares for all God's creatures,
don't he, Vince?
I hope you were never a cunt to him.

VINCENT   No!

PETER   (*To* DEREK, *of* VINCENT.) Was he a cunt?

VINCENT   I wasn't, was I?

DEREK   No, you were alright.

PETER   That girl, Lydia… She's still sending Vince dirty
letters, talking about how she wants him inside her.

Pretty saucy material, actually.
X-rated.

On the news… they're not telling us what's
happening.
They're keeping it quiet.
But it's going fucking nuts all over Essex, Kent,
Cambridgeshire.

They're everywhere.
They're crawling out of the cracks in the earth
Like cockroaches, like earwigs
They're coming out of the sea.

They're dangerous.
And they make *us* feel like shit.
They make *us* feel like we lack something.
That we don't know how to feel.
That we should feel something different.

Pause.

Your feelings are your feelings, Derek.
They are only true.
They are only honest
And God will forgive you.

Pause.

Will you help us?
More and more young people are joining.
You won't be alone.
Girls, too.

Pause. DEREK *nods.* PETER *comes and
embraces him.*

We'll love you, Derek.
We'll love you, as one of us.

Come and find us, tomorrow.
At The Lion.
Two o'clock.

We've got plans, mate.

Pause. PETER *and* VINCENT *exit by the track.*

Pause. DEREK *watches them go.*

He takes VINCENT's *shirt off. He examines his body.*

From the sea-path, SARAH *enters.*

DEREK *turns to her.*

DEREK   How much of that did you hear?

Pause. All of it.

SARAH   We know all about Peter…
We know what he does.
His son… contracted it.
He chucked him out, even though…
Well, he had his own story.

And he went off the rails.
And into fights, drugs.
He used to drive a truck down the A12, picking up girls along the way.
He was lost.

The League turned him.

Pause.

I need to talk about Lydia.
I don't really want you anywhere near us, but it seems I have no choice,

It's too dangerous, here.
There's something happening.
There's chatter.
I'm concerned.

We were supposed to be moving her today.
But she's gone downhill.
She's become very ill.
She isn't responding to the treatment.

I don't think she can go on much longer

Pause.

She's been playing your CD.

The same song over and over.

Pause.

You're a good boy I think, struggling all your
life, not knowing what's it all about.

Even that first time I saw you, I knew you had
courage.

I think it's been growing inside you.
Since that last time.
Blooming.

I can see you shining, Derek.
I can see it in you.

And you can be reborn.

Pause.

Come to her.

DEREK   What can I do?

          I can't do a thing.
          I'm hopeless.

SARAH   Tell her she's alright.
          Just tell her she's alright.

DEREK   Why?

SARAH   If you don't, I think she'll die.

Scene Four

The Miracle

SARAH's *cottage, that night.* LYDIA *is in a chair. The moon is full.*

LYDIA *is listening to a wonderful song from between 1994 and 1997. She looks very ill.*

There are a few lit candles on the table.

DEREK *and* SARAH *have just entered.*

LYDIA *is paler, thinner.* DEREK *approaches.*

LYDIA   I like this song.

DEREK   Yeah?

LYDIA   It's good.

           I used to listen to this song in the car.

           Pause.

           My dad used to play it.

           Pause.

           He 'liked his music'.

DEREK   Sarah asked me to come.

LYDIA   Sarah should leave me alone.

SARAH   Sarah wants you to live.

LYDIA   Sarah's just embarrassing.

           Pause.

           SARAH *leaves* DEREK *and* LYDIA *alone.*

           Pause. LYDIA *turns the music off.*

           You shouldn't have come.

           You come to laugh at me?
           Stare at me again.

DEREK   No.

LYDIA   Then what?

           DEREK *looks at her.*

DEREK   I don't know.

LYDIA   Stare at my mark?

DEREK   No.

LYDIA   You should get out of here before you get
           infected.

DEREK   You won't infect me.

           Pause.

LYDIA   But you fear it?

           Pause.

           How could you betray me?

           Pause.

           It keeps going round and round my head.
           How could you?
           I thought you had such courage.

DEREK   No.

LYDIA   No, no courage.

DEREK   I've never had any.

           I'm no good.

           I'm hardly a person at all.

           I'm not right, I'm... despicable.

           He struggles with this.

           I know that now.

           And if there's anything good to come out of this
           it's that it's set me straight.

           Pause.

           When you came
           I found myself full of dreams.

LYDIA   About what?

DEREK   About you.
And about who I might become.

Pause.

I liked you.

Not just the being beautiful and that, but

But the way you looked for the sea.

And the way you sank into the water, like you
didn't mind the cold.
And the way you seemed to love this place.

And the way something seemed to change
inside me.

And you didn't laugh at me.
You didn't make me feel stupid for having those
dreams.

Pause.

And I felt very strongly that life was beginning

LYDIA   And then I fucked that up

DEREK   No, I

LYDIA   You overheard me, didn't you?

DEREK   It doesn't matter.

LYDIA   Everything I try.

DEREK   You were just being young.

LYDIA   Nasty.

DEREK   It's okay.

LYDIA   So typical of me.

DEREK   It's okay.

LYDIA   Everything I touch.

             DEREK *places his hand on the place where her
mark is.*

DEREK   It's just this.

               It's not you.

               There is something inside me too.
               And it's not me.

               Pause. He keeps his hand there.

LYDIA   I know.

               Pause.

               Did you really like me?

DEREK   I still like you.

LYDIA   How?

DEREK   Of course I do.

               Pause.

LYDIA   (*Of the mark.*) Even with this?

DEREK   Yes.

               Can I see it?

               Pause.

               It's alright, it won't do me harm.

               Pause. She reveals the mark.

               It's okay.

               Pause. DEREK *touches it.*

               It's okay.
               It is what it is.
               There's no harm.

               Pause.

               See.

               Pause. She closes her eyes. He closes his eyes.

               It's just normal.
               We're just normal.

We can just be normal.

Beat. She gets up.

She plays some music from DEREK*'s CD.*

They listen to it.

Pause.

LYDIA   I read your story.

DEREK   What story?

LYDIA   The one about the trawlerman.
          You remember you gave it to me?

          When we first met?

DEREK   Oh yes.

LYDIA   I loved it.

DEREK   Did you?

LYDIA   I thought it was wonderful.

          I felt like you'd really understood his feelings.
          Like you'd got under his skin.

          It was gorgeous.

DEREK   Thank you.

          Pause.

LYDIA   Before Sussex.
          I was at a dance academy in London.
          We felt very free there, all of us.
          Every day we had to have courage.
          To be and feel how we wanted to be.
          To touch others
          To understand the bodies of others.
          It wasn't wrong, it was lovely.
          I felt that I was discovering things every day.

          SARAH *enters, with a slim medical bag.*

          There was a boy called Robbie, and he was my...
          particular friend.

I was fifteen and he was seventeen, and I had sex
with him.
Before the panic.
Before it emerged.
We weren't careful enough.
I was on the pill.

I didn't know that he'd slept with other girls
before me!
We were just young!
Then he got very ill and died.
And other people at the academy.

And then I got very ill.
And my parents
Couldn't handle it.
And started to reject me.
And wouldn't come near me.
And wouldn't hug me.
And that's when it was born inside me.

Pause. She struggles with it.

And one day they were gone.
On a business trip, they said.
And they put me in a hospital.
And they didn't come.
And when the hospital made enquiries
It turned out my mother and father had left
the country.

Pause.

Will you go swimming again, Derek?

DEREK   Yeah.

           Pause. She takes his hand. SARAH *takes a*
           syringe from her bag.

LYDIA   It's time for my medicine.

           LYDIA *nods her head.*
           Then SARAH *injects* LYDIA. *Beat.* SARAH
           recites the liturgy.

SARAH   You've got your heart.
             You've got your heart.
             You've got your blood.
             You've got your blood.
             You've got your wings.
             You know the way.

             Pause. SARAH *goes back inside.* LYDIA *and*
             DEREK. *The sea. The quiet.*

             SARAH *re-enters, with a bottle of wine, and*
             some crisp wine glasses. The bottle is already
             half-drunk, with a cork in it. She looks at them,
             nervously.

             Can I join you?

             Pause. Yes.

             Only half a bottle, but there it is.
             It's English wine.

             She pours them a glass of wine, and hands it
             round.

             This wine was made in the year it first appeared.
             I'm no expert but I'm told it was a very good year.

             Sorry, am I being embarrassing?

             They drink together.

             Do you like it, Derek?

             Pause.

DEREK   Yes, I do.

SARAH   You can taste elderflower.

             Pause. The sea. The wine.

             I used to live in London. I used to be a nurse at
             the Royal Free.
             My husband was a surgeon. He was on the front
             line.

             One day he became very sick, one of the first to
             bloom.

To be perfectly honest, I don't know for sure how he got it.

He died. And then I got it too.
And of course they didn't let me keep my job.
And my friends were afraid to come close to me.
To touch me.
And I began to waste, and fall apart.
And I hated myself.

I wanted to see my family.
This was before the London cordon.

They lived miles away, in Dorset.
I hoped that they might look after me.

I knew I was going home to die.

I got on the train. It was hot, and movement made me feel sick.
And I started vomiting.
And everyone knew.
People wanted me off the train. So I got off, somewhere near Basingstoke
It was a small stop, in the middle of nowhere.
And already quite late.
I did not know where I was but I decided I would just walk.

I was in a lot of pain.
Then night came.
It became dark and cold.
I could not sleep because it was so cold.
And if I had gone to sleep I think I might have died on the road.

In the middle of the night I realised a car was coming.
An old car, a Morris Minor Traveller, you know, with the wooden frame at the back.
But its lights were bright.
I raised my head.
The car began to stop and I was washed with white light.

The car was driven by a beautiful old woman
with white hair.

'Where do you want to go?'
'I want to go home' I said.

We drove for two hours and by the time we got to
my parents' town the sun was rising.
The woman knocked on the old green door and
woke my mother.

Pause.

My mother was bad-tempered, said they couldn't
take me – 'How can we have her here?' She said.
'I can't look after her, how can I?'

I heard the old woman walk slowly back to the
car and open the door and say 'Well then, we
better go'.
And I said 'Where are you taking me?'
And she said 'I'm taking you home.'

As we drove out again she asked me if I wanted
to be reborn and I said 'Yes'.
And she said, 'We can give you some things
which will keep you alive, but to be reborn you
must first reject the loathing inside you...
You are not alone,' she said. And she put her
hands on me. And I felt something changing,
inside me.

Pause.

SARAH *produces some plums, and gives them to*
DEREK *and* LYDIA.

These plums are from the garden.

They're rather sour I'm afraid.

I want you to take all the flesh off the fruit, and
then feel the stone in your mouth.

And put everything you want to get rid of.

All of that inside you. Put it in the stone.

Pause. They do.

All of it.
Now spit it into your hand.

And throw it out to sea. As far as you can.
There. That's done.

Pause.

(*To* DEREK.) Can you stay tonight?

Pause.

DEREK   Yes.

SARAH   It's going to be a difficult few days, I'm afraid.

Pause.

Further down the estuary there have been
disturbances.
There are people in danger, I need to go.

I don't know how long I'll be.

If I'm not back.
You will be collected.

No one knows about this place.
You're quite safe.

And you have each other.

Something's been happening, hasn't it?

Pause.

I think you're very strong.

Pause. She goes to LYDIA.

She gives LYDIA *a hug.*

Whatever happens now, just remember that you
can live.

Pause.

> Look after each other.
> Look after her, Derek.
> Until She comes.
>
> *Pause.*

DEREK   I will.

> SARAH *exits.*

Scene Five

She Will Come One Day

SARAH*'s cottage, a few days later. Late afternoon. Another hot day.*

DEREK *walks up the path with a shopping bag.*

Pause. He throws her a packet of cigarettes. Puts a carton of milk on the table.

LYDIA   Thank you.

> *Pause. She takes out a cigarette and lights it.*

> (*Of the cigarette*.) Tell me not to.

DEREK   No, I won't.

> I'm glad you're feeling up to it.

LYDIA   Yes, I'm feeling up to it.

> I think I'm going to need them, today.

DEREK   Why?

LYDIA   It doesn't matter.

> *Pause.*

> There'll be swimming, where I'm going.
> There'll be a big house
> A big house in the country.

And green hills
And limestone.

Pause.

I'm feeling so much stronger now.

DEREK   I can't believe you're going.

Pause. She smiles. They come close.

You were up in the night.

Are you okay?

LYDIA   Yeah.

Shall we go down to the sea?

DEREK   Yeah.

Pause.

LYDIA   I got you a towel out.

DEREK   Thanks.

LYDIA   And chocolate.

DEREK   Okay.

I can't believe you'll be going.

Pause.

They make contact.

She kisses him on the forehead.

They look at each other. They might kiss.

Would it be different, if I had it?

Pause.

LYDIA *reaches out to him. He reaches back.*
Pause.

LYDIA   In any case, you can't get it from kissing.

Pause. They might.

Pause. They do. Slowly and carefully.

They kiss again.

(*Of the kiss.*) I don't know what this is.

DEREK   No.

LYDIA   This can't last.

DEREK   Why not?

LYDIA   It can't last.

DEREK   I would, you know.
           I'd get it.
           If it would make a difference.

           LYDIA *breaks away.*

LYDIA   Don't say that.

DEREK   Why not?

LYDIA   It's death.

DEREK   It's not.

LYDIA   I could die tomorrow.

DEREK   You won't.

           DEREK *kisses* LYDIA.

           Then VINCENT *enters.*

VINCENT   Whoa!

           They break apart.

           What are you doing?

DEREK   (*Confused, moving towards him.*) Vince.

VINCENT   What were you doing, Derek?

           Pause.

           Oh my god that is

           He recoils.

LYDIA   (*Suddenly worried about* DEREK.) How did you
           find us?

VINCENT   Never mind about that.

LYDIA   Tell me.

VINCENT   The smell of it.

LYDIA   How did you find us?

VINCENT   Satellite maps and hearsay.

            Pause. VINCENT *looks at her.*

            (*Of* LYDIA.) Look at you.

            On the outside you're just as fit as the first
            moment I saw you.

            Pause.

            (*To* LYDIA.) Take your shirt off?

LYDIA   No.

VINCENT   I just want to see

            Will you take your shirt off, please?

            Pause.

            So I know it's real.

            (*Of* DEREK.) That he didn't just make it all up.

DEREK   Vince, stop it.

VINCENT   (*To* LYDIA.) Take it off or I'll make you.

LYDIA   No.

VINCENT   Turn around.

DEREK   Stop it.

VINCENT   Yeah?

DEREK   Or I'll stop you.

VINCENT   (*To* DEREK.) You've never stopped me.
            In all your life, when have you ever?

            (*To* LYDIA.) Turn around, against the window.
            I want to see your face in the reflection.

LYDIA *does nothing*.

We had a thing going, didn't we?
Why did you pull away?
At the last minute?

Beat.

What was wrong with me?

PETER *enters*.

PETER   Oh! Here she is!

DEREK   Peter.

LYDIA   You can't be here.

PETER   You can't be here.
Not on our land.

(*To* LYDIA.) We gave you the warning.

We told you to leave, and you didn't leave.

PETER *gets on his surgical gloves*.

He gets out a knife. The sky is getting dark now.

Derek, mate, I'd like you to go now.
What's about to happen isn't for your eyes.
Just don't worry about it.
You're not part of this.
You're a good boy.
Don't worry about it, mate.
Go on, kid.

You don't need to see this.

DEREK *stares them out*.

DEREK   I won't let it happen.

PETER   She's just a carcass.
I need to cut this at the root, mate.
I need to cut it out, I'm sorry.

Pause.

Don't be soft, son.

You go fall in love with her and she'll only go
and die tomorrow.

DEREK   She will not.

PETER   She'll only go and die.

DEREK   She will not.

LYDIA   I will live.

PETER   She'll die a filthy death.

LYDIA   I will live.

PETER   You'll shrink and waste.
Flies will crawl up your cunt and shit on our
food chain.
You'll pollute the earth.

God told me this, Derek.
God told me I must rid us of her.

What power does she have over you?

VINCENT   She was kissing him.

PETER   Oh my son!

VINCENT   She was sucking the life out of him, poor kid.

PETER   Why were you kissing him?

LYDIA   Because I love him.

PETER   What?

LYDIA   Because I love him.

PETER, *furious turns against her, raises the knife.*

PETER   Love him?

You don't know love.

LYDIA   I do.

PETER *approaches* DEREK, *with his knife.*
DEREK *stands in the way.*

VINCENT   You love him?

LYDIA   (*Conciliatory.*) I'm sorry I turned you away, Vince.

PETER   (*Making to get at her.*) I've had enough of this.

LYDIA   It wasn't about you.

               PETER *makes to get at her, but* DEREK *stands in the way.*

PETER   Let me through.

DEREK   You won't.

PETER   Get away.

               DEREK *pulls his machete out of his bag.*

DEREK   You won't get past me.

               PETER *halts.*

PETER   Get out of the fucking way.

DEREK   (*Of the machete.*) I beat back Sinclair's Way with this.
               I cleared Harcourt's field of ten-foot briars.

PETER   Fuck off or I'll make you regret it.

DEREK   I chopped down a sycamore.

PETER   I'll chop you down in shame.

DEREK   I'm not ashamed.

PETER   I'll make an example of you.

               He lunges but DEREK *raises his blade.* PETER *goes no further.*

               DEREK *and* PETER, *a stand-off.*

               (*Gesturing to him to get* DEREK.) Vincent

               Get him.

VINCENT   What?

               Pause.

PETER   (*Angrily gesturing.*) Get him.

VINCENT   No.

PETER   I said get him, boy.

VINCENT   It's Derek.

            It's Derek, isn't it?

            I've known Derek since the dawn of time.

PETER   What's wrong with you?

VINCENT   There's nothing wrong with me.

PETER   Goodfernothing little / shit.

VINCENT   There's nothing wrong with me, you fucker!

            PETER *tries to control his feelings. He might hit*
            VINCENT.

PETER   (*Praying*.) Oh Father

VINCENT   Oh fuck off.

PETER   Guide me in your / will.

VINCENT   I can't be bothered any / more.

PETER   Show me the way so I can purify this land.

VINCENT   You're a fucking nutter, you are.

            PETER *hits* VINCENT, *sending him spinning off,*
            then he approaches LYDIA.

VINCENT   Pete.

            VINCENT *tries to get in the way again.*

LYDIA   (*To* VINCENT.) It's okay.

VINCENT   (*To* PETER.) Just leave it.

            But now there's only DEREK *in the way.*

LYDIA   Let him come.

            Pause.

Let him come, Derek.
If this is what he must do, let him do it.
I'm not afraid of him.

I know what I am.

You can't hurt me any more.

Pause.

I'm feeling strong.
There's no shame in me.

PETER   No?

LYDIA   *She's* coming for me.

PETER   Fairytales.

LYDIA   Any minute now, she'll come.

Pause.

The sound of a car approaching. PETER *goes to look.*

VINCENT   It's an old Morris!

And now the headlights swing into view, moving across them, illuminating them.

It's an old Morris Minor Traveller, with a wooden frame.

DEREK   A Morris Minor Traveller!

The car stops. The door opens. The headlights remain, casting an extraordinary light on them all.

The OLD LADY *enters.*

They stare at her.

PETER   Who the fuck are you?

OLD LADY   You know who I am.

Pause.

It's over now, Peter.

Put down your blade.

Pause.

It's over.

Pause.

PETER   No, it's not.

Pause. The OLD LADY *pulls out a gun.*

OLD LADY   I was with him
               At the end... Peter.

               He forgave you.
               He understood.
               There was no fear in him.

               He wanted to talk to you.
               He'd tried to call so many times.
               And try to explain to you who he really was.

PETER   I was away.

OLD LADY   He didn't betray you – he was always himself.

               Beat. PETER *winds himself up with this.*

               I saw him die, Peter.

PETER   Where was it?

OLD LADY   At home.

PETER   I chucked him out of home!

OLD LADY   Nonetheless.

               PETER *winds himself up about this.*

               PETER *charges at the* OLD LADY, *but she
               shoots in the air. A warning shot.*

               PETER *stops.*

               Let us be, Peter.

               The things that happened happened.

We've had enough, now.

Pause.

It's time.

All of us.

PETER   (*Of* LYDIA.) Where are you taking her?

OLD LADY   I'm taking her home.

(*To* PETER.) Maybe it's time for you, too.

Pause.

It's over now. Go back home.
Get out of the district.
If we see you again here we'll shoot you.
You'll be dead in a rockpool, do you understand?

The sea will take you.
Go back home.

Pause. PETER *nods. He stumbles off.*

The OLD LADY *turns to* VINCENT.

(*To* VINCENT.) Time for you, too.
When you wake up tomorrow you can start again.

We're going to need you, in the time to come.
Derek's going to need you.

Pause. VINCENT *goes. Pause.*

LYDIA   Where are we going?

OLD LADY   I've got a house.
In Cumbria.

LYDIA   What's it like?

OLD LADY   It's full of light.

Pause.

Are you packed?

Pause.

LYDIA   Yes.

           Beat.

OLD LADY   Is your bag inside?

LYDIA   Yes.

OLD LADY   Then I'll go and get it.

LYDIA   But what about Derek?

           Pause.

OLD LADY   Derek knows what he has to do.

LYDIA   He should come with us.

           Pause.

OLD LADY   Derek's not coming

LYDIA   Why?

OLD LADY   Derek must stay here.

LYDIA   Why?

OLD LADY   Derek belongs here.

LYDIA   Because 'we are who we are and he is who he is'?

OLD LADY   Yes.

LYDIA   I don't accept that.

OLD LADY   You need to be amongst your own.

LYDIA   Why *can't* he come?

OLD LADY   You're young.

LYDIA   Yes. And I have a future.

OLD LADY   Yes.

LYDIA   I'm young. I have a future.

           I just want him in the car.

OLD LADY   Why?

LYDIA   We're going swimming.

               Take him, as far as he wants to go.

               The OLD LADY *smiles. She considers.*

               A long pause.

OLD LADY   (*To* DEREK.) Do you want to come?

DEREK   Yes.

OLD LADY   You don't say it lightly?

DEREK   No.

               Pause.

OLD LADY   I'll go and get the bags.

               Pause. The OLD LADY *exits. The two of them.*

LYDIA   In Cumbria, there are waterfalls
               And pools
               And hills.

               Pause.

               I made you a CD.

               Pause.

               He smiles. She gets it out. Gives it to him.

               It was going to be as a goodbye, but
               We can play it in the car.

DEREK   What's on it?

LYDIA   Nineties.

               Pause. He takes the CD.

DEREK   You wrote it all out!

LYDIA   Yeah.

               Pause. DEREK *looks at the track list.*

DEREK   (*Of the* OLD LADY.) I'm not sure this'll be her
               kind of thing.

They laugh. The OLD LADY *re-emerges.*

OLD LADY   Are you ready?

LYDIA   Yes.

Pause.

Where *are* we going?

The OLD LADY *takes the bags in the direction of her car. She turns to look back at them.*

OLD LADY   We're going home.

LYDIA *turns and follows her off.*

Pause. DEREK *watches as they get in the car.*

He turns to look at his land. Then he too goes to the car.

The ignition. A door slams. The car reverses and the headlights sweep over the cottage. An intensity of bright light. The car drives off.

A Nick Hern Book

Crushed Shells and Mud first published as a paperback original in Great Britain in 2015 by Nick Hern Books Limited, The Glasshouse, 49a Goldhawk Road, London W12 8QP, in association with Strickland Productions Ltd

Cover image: Alex Rafael Rose

Designed and typeset by Nick Hern Books, London
Printed in the UK by Mimeo Ltd, Huntingdon, Cambridgeshire PE29 6XX

A CIP catalogue record for this book is available from the British Library

ISBN   978 1 84842 531 6

www.nickhernbooks.co.uk

facebook.com/nickhernbooks

twitter.com/nickhernbooks